从备课开始的

56 个

英语创意教学

快速从小白老师到名师高手

丁仁仑 /（澳）珍妮·沃恩 (Janienne Vaughan) 著

中国青年出版社 CHINA YOUTH PRESS

图书在版编目（CIP）数据

从备课开始的56个英语创意教学：快速从小白老师到名师高手/丁仁仑，（澳）珍妮·沃恩著.
—北京：中国青年出版社，2020.7
ISBN 978-7-5153-5987-8

Ⅰ.①从… Ⅱ.①丁… ②珍… Ⅲ.①英语—教学研究 Ⅳ.①H319.3

中国版本图书馆CIP数据核字（2020）第042749号

从备课开始的56个英语创意教学：
快速从小白老师到名师高手

作 者	丁仁仑 （澳）珍妮·沃恩
责任编辑	周 红
美术编辑	佟雪莹
出 版	中国青年出版社
发 行	北京中青文文化传媒有限公司
电 话	010-65511272/65516873
公司网址	www.cyb.com.cn
购书网址	zqwts.tmall.com
印 刷	大厂回族自治县益利印刷有限公司
版 次	2020年7月第1版
印 次	2022年11月第4次印刷
开 本	787×1092 1/16
字 数	286千字
印 张	18
书 号	ISBN 978-7-5153-5987-8
定 价	49.90元

版权声明

思维导图

Mind-Maps

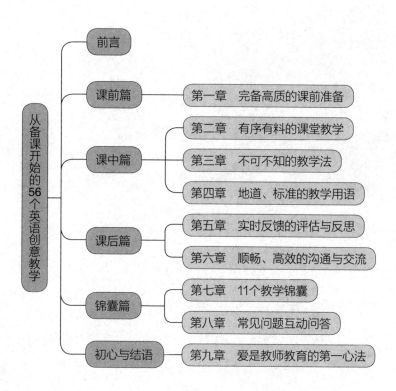

从备课开始的56个英语创意教学

- 前言
- 课前篇 —— 第一章　完备高质的课前准备
- 课中篇 —— 第二章　有序有料的课堂教学
  - 第三章　不可不知的教学法
  - 第四章　地道、标准的教学用语
- 课后篇 —— 第五章　实时反馈的评估与反思
  - 第六章　顺畅、高效的沟通与交流
- 锦囊篇 —— 第七章　11个教学锦囊
  - 第八章　常见问题互动问答
- 初心与结语 —— 第九章　爱是教师教育的第一心法

目 录

Contents

第三章　不可不知的教学法

第四章　地道、标准的教学用语

第三部分 **课后篇 After Teaching**   163

第五章 实时反馈的评估与反思
In & After Class – Assessment and Reflection   164

第七章　11个教学锦囊

第八章　常见问题互动问答

前 言

Preface

本书基于我和珍妮女士自身多年的教学经验以及对新入职场的少儿英语教师培训经历编写而成，旨在为英语教师提供一本简洁、实用的教学手册，帮助教师尽快适应教师角色，快速进入教学程序，迅速提升教学技能，加速职业晋升，在短时间内成为有创意的高效能英语骨干教师。

本书主要特点有：

• **生动有趣的实践案例，拿来即用，一用有效**

24个精彩的教学案例故事呈现了高效能教师的教育理念、教学方法、教学手段；32个教学模板或素材资源，提供了直接可用或可参考借鉴的教案、图表、检查单、档案袋以及学生成绩报告和与家长沟通的电邮等文件。

• **中英双语，教学技能和语言水平双提高**

本书部分内容直接引用一线资深外教地道、纯正的英文教案和模板，以便教师学习，或直接拿来用于教学实践。为便于理解，部分内容用中文阐述。教师在提高英语教学技能的同时，还能提升英语教学中地道的英语表达能力。

• **每章后附有小结、反思和练习模块，以便教师学以致用**

教师在研读教学案例、教学理论后，可参考每章后所附的小结、反思和练习模块，与自己的教学实践相结合，尝试设计自己的教学计划。其中还有特别设计的教研团队集体讨论与分享练习，以供教研团队开展主题性教研活动，共同提高教学水平。

- **既循序渐进，环环相扣，又各自成章**

全书以课前、课中、课后为时间轴，不仅讲述了24个教学案例故事，提供了32个教学素材或模板，还单独成章分别阐述了9个实用的教学法、9类地道纯正的课堂教学用语、10大常用的心理效应，以及11条教学锦囊妙计。

全书分为五个部分。第一部分为课前准备篇，即第一章。主要内容是走上讲台之前的课前准备，内容包括制定教学计划和目标，写备课教案，做好教学准备。特别提供了国际学校少儿英语教案、国内重点小学英语教案、初中英语教案和高中英语教案示范以供参考。

第二部分为课堂教学篇，分别用三章来进行阐述。第二章通过教学案例故事的简述，提供了10个有料有趣的课堂管理法。第三章则对当前教育界最热点的9个先进教学法做了专业的解读和运用指导。第四章提供的是地道、标准、常用的课堂教学用语。

第三部分为课后篇，包括第五章和第六章。第五章为评估与反思，主要展述评估的方式、方法、手段以及课后反思的重要性。第六章重点阐述沟通交流的方式、方法及交流要点，并同步介绍了10个对沟通交流十分有益的心理效应理论。

第四部分为锦囊篇，包括第七章和第八章。第七章提供了行之有效的11条教学锦囊妙计；第八章为常见问题互动问答，列举了几个比较常见又容易被人忽略或误会的教学概念，并做了简略解答。

第五部分为初心与结语，即第九章。作者用三个教学故事，分享对教之初心的理解——爱与责任。只要出于爱与责任，就会守护孩子安全，有耐心，想方设法激励并帮助孩子健康成长。

作者均为一线教师，对于教师工作的忙碌非常理解并感同身受。因此，书中内容力求简明扼要，用具体的教学故事、模板、案例、素材、资源，直接给出教学各环节的示范样本及教学心法，供参考借鉴或直接使用。

本书适用于中小学校、国际学校和教育培训机构的年轻英语教师，也对从事英语教育有经验的教师、英语课程设计研发人员、教育管理者有一定的参考借鉴作用，对关心孩子英语启蒙教育的宝妈、宝爸等家长朋友们来说，也可阅读参考。

有人说，A mediocre teacher tells; a good teacher explains; a superior teacher demonstrates; the BEST teacher inspires.（普通的老师教知识;好老师答疑解惑；优秀的老师示范演示；最好的老师激发激励。）我们认为，高效能的教师既会传道授业、答疑解惑、示范演示，亦擅长启发激励学生（*A highly effective teacher tells, explains, demonstrates and inspires*）。

愿本书的讲述、阐释、示范，给予您启发和激励，对您有所裨益！

衷心地祝愿您阅读愉快！

丁仁仑

珍妮·沃恩

2020年3月28日于中国杭州、新加坡

课 前 篇
Before Teaching

第一章
完备高质的课前准备
Before Class: Planning and Preparation

"美好的一天始于前一天晚上"。所有高质量的有效教学均源于充分细致的提前准备（*The old adage "A good day starts the night before" can be applied to teaching since effective teaching always begins with thoughtful preparation*）。我们看到即使很有经验的教师，也会提前花上一两个小时甚至更多时间把教室布置好，认真地写好画好板书；他们把教案写好后，一遍又一遍地在脑海里演示教学的各个环节。The mental activity involved in pre-thinking through a lesson is usually greater than any written lesson plan, although producing a lesson plan can ensure that some thought has been undertaken.

首先，了解学生的现有水平非常重要（*The first task is to ascertain what your students know*）。可以通过前任教师了解学生的学情，当然也可以通过上课来迅速了解学生。要做到这一点不一定非要通过考试。做个好玩的自我介绍游戏，说个字母让他们写在白板上，一起读个故事再让他们画出来，这些都可以用来了解他们的语言水平。

方法一：

Playing a circle game of introducing themselves through a repetitious chant can quickly show the students who are confident in speaking and have some basic knowledge of English greetings. For example: My name is Mrs. Janienne. What is your name? My name is Andrew. What is your name?

方法二：

Asking students to write the letter for the sound that you say in a team game on whiteboards can be used to assess students' knowledge of letter sounds and where you should begin teaching.

方法三：

Reading a story together and then asking students to draw the story will also show those students who are comprehending the language.

Once you have ascertained where your students are at, you need to set clear goals. Develop a plan for the next few weeks or a semester to cover what you feel your students need to learn in their English journey. Your plan may be to teach all the single letter sounds within the next eight weeks; or it may be to write simple meaningful sentences and to read with understanding books at a particularly level.

其次，确定学生的学习水平和情况之后，就是制定教学目标和教学计划。当然，你的目标和计划要符合学校或机构的课程要求。（ *Of course, your goals will need to fit into the curriculum framework of the school or learning center with which you are attached.* ）

下面的表格呈现了清晰的教学目标，能基本满足大多数的课程大纲要求。The following table, co-constructed by the author, presents some clear objectives, which would fit most curricula:

表1 总体教学目标

Table 1: Language Learning Outcomes

表1一般用于学校或课程的总体教学目标。

LISTENING: Students will be able to show their understanding by:
a) identifying basic personal details. (name, age, etc.)
b) following simple instructions, commands and directions.
c) listening with sustained concentration in different contexts to build new banks of words.

SPEAKING: Students will be able to show their understanding by:
a) naming concrete objects and using functional vocabulary.
b) repeating words, phrases, tongue twisters and poems.
c) answering questions in single words or short phrases.
d) communicating personal and survival needs appropriately.

READING: Students will be able to show their understanding by:
a) matching sounds to letters and words.
b) reading and understanding words, phrases and simple sentences with visual clues.
c) answering recall questions about the text.

WRITING: Students will be able to show their understanding by:

a) forming letters and copying words.

b) using knowledge of sound-symbol relationships to initiate spelling skills.

c) beginning to use high-frequency words to write short sentences.

听：学生的理解力可以通过以下内容得以展示：

1）能确定基本的个人信息，比如性别、名字、年龄

2）能听懂基本指令、命令和方向

3）在不同语境下能保持听的注意力并学会一些新词

说：学生的理解力可以通过以下内容得以展示：

1）能说出具体的物品，会用功能动词

2）能重复词和短语、绕口令、诗歌

3）能用简单的词或短语来回答问题

4）能够恰当表达个人生活需求

读：学生的理解力可以通过以下内容得以展示：

1）能把发音和字母及单词连线配对

2）在视觉线索的提示下能读出并理解词、短语和简单句子。

3）能回答与课文有关的复述性问题

写：学生的理解力可以通过以下内容得以展示：

1）能拼出字母，抄写单词

2）能用音形的关系来建立拼写技能

3）能开始用高频词写短句子

表1的教学目标有些宽泛，一般是作为学校课程的目标来陈述的。作为教师，还需要制定详细的具体教学计划以实现上表中的大目标。制定之前，请参考表2——制定完美教学计划的框架。

These broad objectives need to be fleshed out. How will they get to each of these points? What will the process be? Where will you begin? What will you centre your lessons around? Thinking through these questions will be time well spent in making lessons that are effectual. The framework below may be useful for effective planning.

表2 制定完美教学计划的框架
Table 2: Framework for Perfect Planning[①]

1	Aims
2	Objectives
3	Assessment data on pupils
4	Scope and content
5	Pedagogical methods
6	Teacher's expectations
7	Learning activities
8	Homework
9	Differentiation of Learning
10	Progression in learning
11	Other curricular links
12	Time

① Anthony Haynes. *The Complete Guide to Lesson Planning and Preparation*. London: Continuum. 2010. P168.

13	Space
14	Resources
15	Languages
16	Ancillary staff
17	Risks
18	Assessment
19	Evaluation method(s)
20	Review procedure(s)

　　表2可供课前准备、制定教学计划时作参考，也可以当作检查单（checklist）来检查教学计划制定得是否全面。

　　You may feel that these aims and objectives are confusing. Here is a simple explanation, which is enough for now. Generally speaking, goals and aims are large-scale, overall aims applying to the curriculum. "Objectives are similar to aims in that they specify what you are trying to achieve in a lesson or sequence of lessons. They differ in that they are narrow and more specific."[1] As for outcomes, they are "based on objectives providing teachers and students with measures of progress towards goals".[2]

　　再次，众所周知，语言是由多项相互联系的技能组成，比如听、说、读、写、译等。这些组成元素或宏观技能也理应融入课堂教学中，正如它们在现实交流中同时被使用一样。因此，学生在学习时要掌握听、说、

---

① Anthony Haynes. *The Complete Guide to Lesson Planning and Preparation*. London: Continuum. 2010. P67.

② Peter Mickan. *Language Curriculum Design and Socialisation*. Toronto: Multilingual matters. 2013. P46.

读、写等语言技能；老师在教学时要鼓励学生多运用各种感官功能，哪怕只是学某个音或字母。这些语言宏观技能不应该被割裂开来单独教授，而是应该综合教授。

通常，每个人会运用自己的多个感官来学习吸收知识与信息。有些人的某一感官略强于其他感官，于是就会越来越依赖于该感官。然而，如果我们用更多的感官来学习和吸收知识与信息，效果就会更好，记忆周期就会更长久。

多感官学习方法的效果，近年来已被诸多研究所证实。因此，教师应尽可能运用该教学方法，从而更好地针对不同学习风格的学生开展教学。

For example, we visually display the letter we are learning. Then we say the sound it makes clearly for students to hear. Next we encourage students to repeat it so they are saying it. They could perhaps make a body movement to go with it. Finally, we ask them to write the letter so that they feel the sound. Four of the five senses have thus been activated.

Stories have a larger vocabulary than spoken language and therefore, by exposing students to stories, we build their vocabulary and also the interrelated contextual use of the words in dynamic sentences. Consequently, I would plan to integrate stories into my lessons as often as possible.

The stories can also be presented in the form of songs, poetry and tongue twisters. The rhythm and rhyme of this form of language can help students with their memorization of vocabulary as well as with articulation and clarity of speech. Songs, especially, seem to be very useful in accessing the long-term memory of our brains. Therefore, it can be a powerful tool for expanding vocabulary.

To be effective, a teacher should develop an understanding of how long an activity should take. Adding up the time given for each activity will help you to be able to pace yourself through the lesson. Of course, this is a skill which develops with experience. Nevertheless, a beginning teacher is advised to think through the amount of time an activity should take without it being too rushed. In my view it is better to plan more activities and to not get through everything, instead of planning not enough and having extra time that you don't know what to do with.

教师要想方设法激励学生参与各种学习体验，而不是单纯地、机械地抄写或重复某些个单词或音节，从而帮助学生积极、活跃地利用多感官来学习。

被动地学习只是一只耳朵进，另一只耳朵出，效果当然不如积极主动学习。(*Learning is never effective as a passive activity for that is when information goes "in one ear and out the other".*) Instead, students must be encouraged to think. They should be challenged to analyse, synthesize, compare, contrast and display their thinking. Lessons should be planned to get students thinking and doing, not just the teacher doing all of the thinking.

最后，认真备课，写好教案，对成功的课堂教学是最重要的。语言是听、说、读、写等多项相互联系的技能组成的。教学目标要清晰，通过让学生多感官体验达成教学目标；而这种多感官体验务必要激励学生积极参与。(*In summary, careful planning is paramount for a successful lesson. Clearly thought out objectives are planned to be achieved through multi-sensory experiences, which engage a student's brain in active learning.*)

表3是一周教学计划，供参考。The following plans may not be perfect, but they could be helpful guides.

表3　一周教学计划

Table 3: Planning & Observations

How We Organize Ourselves (Food systems to meet needs)

Week 6　16th–20th September

	Tuesday Period 4 (11:00 – 11:50)	Thursday Period 1 (8:10 – 9:00)	Friday Period 1 (10:10 – 11:00)
Objectives	1. to say the days of the week clearly. 2. to read and write the letters b, c and f. 3. to speak in sentences.	1. to articulate a song clearly. 2. to read and write the letters d and g. 3. to expand vocabulary. 4. to understand a process.	1. to articulate words clearly. 2. to read and write the letters a, b, c, d, e, f, g, h, i, l, o, r, t, u. 3. to blend letters to make words. 4. to expand vocabulary.
Activities	Review the days of the week, using the calendar. Quickly review single sounds: h, r, a, e u, l, i, t, o with children writing them on whiteboards. Review the short vowels. Play a game identifying them in words.	Sort and glue Words Their Way spelling into their books, reviewing letters d and g. Make toffee apples together. Read the recipe aloud and ask the students to do the steps with support.	Review the days of the week, using the calendar. Review single letters taught so far, esp. b, c and f and the vowels, writing them on the small whiteboards. Blend them into words and write these in their books, e.g. big, go, fat, cat, bad, dog, bag, etc.

	Tuesday Period 4 (11:00 – 11:50)	Thursday Period 1 (8:10 – 9:00)	Friday Period 1 (10:10 – 11:00)
Activities	Teach the letters b, d, f, c and g. Write them in their books, saying the sounds as they write. Draw pictures of things beginning with these letters. Write labels for each one. If time permits, teach the song "*Toffee Apples.*"	Children cut and paste the pictures in the correct order as we go through the process. Review the process through their pictures.	Sequence pictures and talk about the process of making toffee apples. Match sentences to each picture. Glue them into their books. Re-read the process. Sing the song "*Toffee Apples*".
Plenary	Find the letters b, c, d, g and f in their booklets.	Sing the song "*Toffee Apple*". Point to each word as we sing it.	Sing the song "*Toffee Apples*".
Observations			Next week: Field Trip = Thursday 26th Sept 8:30 – lunchtime. (need to change G2.1 push-in)

教案示范

有了课程目标，制定了每周教学计划，下面来看几个具体教案。

先来一盘"好吃的果冻"。想不到吧，一边吃还可以一边进行科学探究。

1. 科学探究课教案

Lesson plan 1: I Like Jelly – Based on an Inquiry into Scientific Matter

本课将探究物质属性及它们的变化，培养学生书写叙事能力。

This lesson may form part of an inquiry into the properties of matter and how they change.

It can be used to develop children's ability to describe substances and to write procedural texts.

教学目标：学习使用描述性词语

学习表达一系列事件

学习用祈使动词写说明书

Objectives: to use descriptive vocabulary

to express a sequence of events

to write instructions using imperative verbs (bossy language)

课堂活动 Learning Activities：

根据班级人数的多少准备适量的水晶果冻。我通常是给四到六个学生准备一盒果冻。每一组配备一个碗、一个调羹、一个量杯。给每个组不同颜色的果冻。同时你还需要开水和冷水，还有电冰箱。

Depending on the size of the class, obtain packets of jelly crystals. I would suggest one packet per four to six students. Each group would also need a bowl, a spoon and a measuring cup. Use a different coloured jelly crystal for each group. You will also need access to boiling water and cold water as well as a refrigerator.

步骤 Steps：

Step 1：Open the packet of jelly crystals (jello) into a bowl so every child can observe them closely.

Step 2：Discuss what they can see. Write descriptive words on a chart or board as they are used. Encourage students to use their senses. What does it look like? Does it have any smell? What does it feel like?

Step 3：Encourage students to speak a sentence about the jelly crystals to a partner. (This step uses the "Think, Pair, Share" work routine.)

Step 4：Boil a jug of water. Again, discuss what they see using their senses and write descriptive words on the chart or board.

Step 5：Each group pours one cup of boiling water onto the jelly crystals. Ask the students to describe what has happened. Add more descriptive words to their chart.

Step 6 : Ask the students to take turns stirring the mixture until the jelly crystals are completely dissolved.

Step 7 : Add a cup of cold water. Then place the bowl of jelly into a refrigerator.

Step 8 : Review the process with the students drawing pictures for each step on a graphic organizer worksheet. (See attached.)

Step 9 : Then discuss what action happened for each step, writing the imperative verb on the board. Ask students to complete the sentence for each step beginning with the listed verb.

复习巩固 Review：

Look at the jelly and describe it. How has it changed?

Read their procedural text to another person. Identify the imperative verbs. Also identify any descriptive vocabulary. Can they add any more descriptive words to their instructions?

后续活动巩固 Follow Up Lesson Activities：

Look at the set jelly and discuss what it looks like.

Put some on a plate and observe its different properties comparing it to the jelly crystals.

Teach the poem, *"Jelly on a Plate"*.

How To Make Jelly

```
┌─────────┐          _____
│         │          _____
│         │          _____
└────┬────┘          _____
     ▼
┌─────────┐          _____
│         │          _____
│         │          _____
└────┬────┘
     ▼
┌─────────┐          _____
│         │          _____
│         │          _____
└────┬────┘
     ▼
┌─────────┐          _____
│         │          _____
│         │          _____
└─────────┘          _____
```

Jelly on a Plate

Jelly on a plate..

Jelly on a plate..

Wibble, wobble, wibble, wobble,

Jelly on a plate..

一起吃果冻吧！发给学生一次性纸杯和调羹。

Eat the jelly with the students. (I would give each child a small serving in a paper cup with a disposable spoon.)

As they eat it, I would sing the song, "*I like Jelly*", a song which I learnt over forty years ago. (There is a clap at each *.)

Write sentences about the jelly, complete sentence starters or do a cloze exercise using the words of the poem or the song.

Share their sentences before singing the song again.

(I would encourage the students to take home the words of the song and the poem.)

I Like Jelly①

I like jelly –

    wobbly, delicious* jelly.

I like jelly –

    wobbly, delicious* jelly.

Nice, yummy flavours –

    orange, red and green.

Jelly, oh jelly –

    Eat too much; get a pain in the tummy.

Sometimes you can't, you just can't resist –

A nice, big helping of* jelly.

I like jelly –

    wobbly, delicious* jelly②.

① The song, "*I Like Jelly*" comes from a now out-of-print songbook, which I purchased over 40 years ago. The source of the lyrics are unknown.
② I have used this song repeatedly in my long teaching career and have developed my own worksheets based on the song, like the one above. The tune is quite jazzy and syncopated. In order to help the children to capture the rhythm, I taught them to do one clap at each * symbol.

吃完果冻，我们接着来开汽车——主题类教案并不难，让我们一起来唱这首"*Take you riding in my car, car*"！

2. 主题类教案

Lesson Plan 2: The Car – Based on a Theme

这个主题可以制定一周课程的教案，也可以只用来制定一次课的教案。

The theme may be for as long as one week or just one lesson.

Here is a lesson plan centred around a car.

教学目标：扩展词汇量

学会读写 /ar/

写出有意义的句子

理解故事

Objectives: to expand vocabulary

to read and write the digraph /ar/

to write meaningful sentences

to comprehend a story

课堂活动 Learning Activities：

集体制作小汽车。每6个人一组，制作一辆车。你可以先用粉笔在黑板或用彩笔在画板上画出车的大致轮廓。

步骤 Steps :

Step 1 : Build a large car as a group activity. Make more cars, if the class has more than six students. You may choose to draw a big outline of a car with chalk in a playground or on a cement surface. I have also done this on carpet, as the chalk will rub off in time.

Step 2 : Discuss: How do we write the word "car"?

Step 3 : Ask the children to write the word "car" many times all over their car. Ensure every child writes the word a couple of times, as this will help them to learn the word.

Step 4 : Discuss what sounds they hear in the word, "car". Teach them that the letters "a" and "r" go together to make the sound /ar/.

Step 5 : Ask the children to put a line under each of the "ar" letters in the word car, like this: c<u>ar</u>.

How many /ar/ phonograms did they underline?

Step 6 : Allow the children to have a short play in their car as you sing the song: "*Take you riding in my car, car*".

Take you riding in my car, car

Take you riding in my car, car

Take you riding in my car, car

Take you riding in my car

Step 7 : Talk about what a car can do. (It can take you to places. You can drive it. It can make you go to sleep.)

Step 8 : Model writing some sentences using the following sentence starters: The words in brackets are just suggestions for what to write; but allow the students to suggest their ideas.

We made ………….. (a big car).

It had ………….. (four wheels and a steering wheel).

The car could ………….. (move slowly).

I liked ………….. (sitting in it).

Step 9 : Erase the endings that you modelled and just leave the sentence starters. Ask the students to write their own sentences. This will encourage students to not simply copy your work but to engage in their own thinking. Move around the class, assisting various students with this task individually.

复习巩固 Review ：

What have we learnt today? Can you find any other words that use the phonogram /ar/? List some, e.g. *far, farm, bar, card, start, star.*

Sing the song again as they leave.

后续活动巩固 Follow Up Lesson Activities:

Read "*Mr Gumpy's Motor Car*" by John Burningham. (This story is available for viewing on YouTube.)

Look at the verbs in the story, e.g. *pushed, etc.* Teach -ed phonogram as the past tense ending.

Change the tense of the story.

主题类教案很常用，下面来看看动物主题类教案——"*I'm a Great Big Tiger*"。

3. 动物主题类教案

Lesson Plan 3: I'm a Great Big Tiger (trad.) – Based on a Theme

本主题教学可以持续一周或六周。本教案围绕老虎、丛林展开，请充分运用想象力。

The theme may be for as long as one week or six weeks.

Here is a lesson plan centered around Tigers, Jungle or Using Your Imagination.

教学目标：扩展词汇

写出富有意义的句子

能够清晰地发音

能正确解释缩写形式

Objectives: to expand vocabulary

to write meaningful sentences

to articulate words clearly

to explain contractions correctly

课堂活动 Learning Activities：

建议用于2—6岁学龄儿童，主要看学生的语言水平。

（*2 to 6 years old, depends on the learner's English language proficiency*）

步骤 Steps：

Step 1：Show a picture of a tiger.

I'm a great, big tiger.①

By Zoe McHenry

I'm a great big tiger,
creeping through the jungle.
I've great big teeth
and long sharp claws.
I'm creeping through the jungle.

———————————

① Zoe McHenry. *The Useful Book: Songs and Ideas from Play School.* Sydney: ABC Books. 1988.

Step 2：Can they be tigers? (This is dependent upon the age of the students.)

Step 3：Sing the song, "*I'm a Great Big Tiger*", while pretending to be a tiger.

Step 4 : Discuss what it is, where it lives, what it is like and what it does, while writing labels of important vocabulary on the picture.

Step 5 : Ask the students to complete the following sentences:

I'm a great, big _____.

I creep through the _____.

I have big _____ *and long, sharp* _____.

Step 6 : Ask students to illustrate their sentences to show that they link meaning to the vocabulary.

Step 7 : Sing the song a few times again with the children until they know it. Use actions and perhaps finish with a big roar.

Step 8 : Draw the children's attention to the word "I'm". Ask them what it means? Why don't we sing or say "I a great big tiger"? What is the letter "m" doing after the word "I"? (Accept ideas.)

Step 9 : If necessary, state your own name using this construction, i.e. I'm Mrs. Vaughan.

I'm a teacher. I'm happy today. I'm hungry.

Step 10 : Explain that it is short for "I'm". This is called a contraction. It is when we push two words together and make them into one word. Use "I'm" in a few sentences. Ask the children to say their names using the contraction, I'm (Mei Mei), and perhaps another sentence, e.g. *I'm a girl / boy.*

Ask the children if they can find the other contraction in the song.

(I've)

Step 11 : What two words is this contraction made up of?

"*I've great big, teeth*" means the same as "*I have great, big teeth*".

Model another sentence that is true for you, e.g. "*I've black hair*" or "*I've two eyes*".

Step 12 : Encourage the children to suggest other sentences for themselves.

Step 13 : Challenge the children to find other contractions in some books. A contraction is often used in speech so we can say words quickly.

复习巩固 Review :

Tell me a contraction. What is a contraction?

Sing the song again. Are they articulating their words well?

Read the story "*Into the Jungle*" by Judy Hindley or watch the YouTube trailer, "*The Fantastic Jungles of Henri Rousseau*".

后续活动巩固 Follow Up Lesson Activities :

In a following lesson, discuss other animals. Make a list of their names, how they move, where they live and what they have. This could be done together on a poster or whiteboard.

表4可用于本教案的后续教学活动互动环节，让学生讨论一下其他动物。也完全可以根据学生的认知和他们的英语水平来调整设计不同的讨论内容。

表4 动物

Table 4: About Animals

Name of animal	How it moves	Where it lives	Two things it has
Tiger	creeps	jungle	teeth, claws
Zebra	runs	grassland	stripes, long legs
Dolphin	dives	ocean	smooth skin, small eyes

唱首歌，使用这些信息创作新的诗句，用所提供的歌曲模板编写一首新的歌词。鼓励学生自己写出新的诗歌来描述他们认识的不同动物有何不同之处。

Sing the song, using this information for new verses.

Model writing a new verse using the template below.

Encourage the children to write their own new verses. Can they think of a different animal?

My Song :

       I'm a _____ ,

       _____ .

       I've _____

       and _____ .

       I'm _____ .

Conclude the lesson by singing the new verses and compiling their pages into a new booklet.

有时，我们还需要稍微加工改编，比如教案4。这可是教介词的好范例!

4. 故事改编教案

Lesson Plan 4: "My Cat Likes to Hide in Boxes" – Based on the Book by Eve Sutton

由Eve Sutton著Lynley Dodd绘画的经典儿童故事书*My Cat Likes to*

Hide in Boxes[①]由企鹅图书1973年出版。来自不同国家的猫咪们做着怪诞奇异的事儿，但是这只寻常的猫咪却喜欢躲在盒子里。网上可以找到这本书，还有儿歌版。（*The classic book "My Cat Likes to Hide in Boxes" by Eve Sutton and illustrated by Lynley Dodd, was first published in 1973 by Penguin Books. Cats from different countries do strange and exotic things, but this ordinary cat likes to hide in boxes. It is also available on the internet in a read-along format and in a song version.*）

教学目标：了解介词

说出有意义的句子

理解故事

阅读并探讨韵律

Objectives: to understand preposition vocabulary

to speak in meaningful sentences

to comprehend a story

to read and explore rhyme

---

① Author: Eve Sutton, Illustrator: Lynley Dodd. 1973. "My Cat Likes to Hide in Boxes" Publisher: Penguin Books.

课堂活动 Learning Activities：

教学材料准备：一只玩具猫、几个不同的纸盒子、带有介词的闪卡、课堂活动工作表。

Resources: a soft toy cat, a few different boxes, flashing cards with prepositions, activity worksheet

步骤 Steps：

Step 1：Introduce a soft toy cat to the class. Does anyone know what this is called in English? Discuss their experiences of cats.

Step 2：(Have a few different boxes available around the room.) Hide the toy cat and ask the children to find it. Whoever finds the cat may have a turn to hide it again.

Step 3：Introduce the prepositions "in", "on", "under", "behind", "beside", "above" to the children. (Write these words on flashcards before the lesson.) Demonstrate these words to the children using the cat and one of the boxes. Then ask the children to pretend to be a cat and pretend that their chair has a big box on it. As you hold up a word and say it, the children must get into the correct position.

Step 4：Continue to play this position game without saying the position words, so that the students are encouraged to read the word for themselves.

Step 5：Following this activity, gather the children around you seated in a circle, with one of the boxes and the cat in the centre of them. Then ask the children to tell you where the cat is as you hold it in different positions. Encourage them to speak using the sentence: The cat is _____ the box.

Step 6 : As this is known, ask children to complete the worksheet. (See *My Cat Likes to Hide in Boxes* position booklet.) Alternatively, the student could draw different positions on a box and write captions to go with each drawing using the preposition words.

Step 7 : Finally read the book to the children or play the song to them.

复习巩固 Review：

Do a quick review of the preposition words, asking the children to put their hands in different positions.

后续活动巩固 Follow Up Lesson Activities：

Listen to the story / song again.

Look at a map with the children, show them the different countries. Review what the cats did in each country.

Ask different students to hold a sign of the different countries and then act out what each cat did at the particular place.

Discuss how can they remember which cat does what.

Introduce the concept of rhyme – words ending with the same sounds.

Finish the activity worksheet, match countries and words with the correct cat picture. Then complete the missed rhyming word activity.

复习巩固 Review:

最后，再唱一遍这首歌。

Finally, sing the song once again.

下表是本课教学用表，可以在课堂教学中使用，也可以用于复习环节。

The worksheets below accompany this lesson.

My Cat Likes to Hide in Boxes[1]

Match and draw a line.

Brazil		police
Greece		fan
France		violin
Japan		doorway
Berlin		aeroplane
Norway		dance
Spain		chill

[1] The author has created these worksheets based on this classic book, using pictures from the actual book. The pictures in the worksheets are very important for students to be able to connect with the story and their learning. Therefore, the two worksheets must be given at the same time, perhaps printed back-to-back allowing students' quick and easy reference to the pictures as well as the text.

Rhyme!

The cat from Fr_____.

Liked to sing and _____.

The cat from Sp_____.

Flew an _____.

The cat from Br_____.

Caught a very bad _____.

The cat from B_____.

Played the _____.

The cat from N_____.

Got stuck in the _____.

The cat from Gr_____.

Joined the _____.

The cat from J_____.

Waved a big blue _____.

示范：

My Cat Likes to Hide in Boxes Position Booklet

　　请把以下文字打印出来，做成与后面图片匹配的文字大小，让学生进行配对练习。

The cat is behind the box.

The cat is beside the box.

The cat is below the box.

The cat is above the box.

The cat is inside the box.

The cat is in front of the box.

Answers to Rhyme:

The cat from France liked to sing and dance;

The cat from Spain flew an aeroplane;

The cat from Brazil caught a very bad chill;

The cat from Berlin played violin;

The cat from Norway got stuck in the doorway;

The cat from Greece joined the police;

The cat from Japan waved a big blue fan.

1.

2.

3.

4.

5.

6.

教学分为课前、课中和课后。课中是教学环节的关键部分，因为所有的课前准备和课后评估与反思均服务于课中，也就是课堂教学。这也是我们在教案制定这个环节不吝笔墨的用意。根据孩子的年龄、认知能力以及制定的课程教学目标，课堂教学可以分为开场（Warm-up）、课堂教学（Teaching）、结尾（Closure）部分。也可以按自己的教学设计进一步细化，如：

Part 1：Greetings / Warm-up Activities / Pre-teaching

Part 2：Teaching / Learning Activities

Part 3：Review

Part 4：Follow up Lesson Activities

Part 5：Closure

教学活动的设计要符合学生年龄阶段的特点。如少儿英语阶段，唱儿歌开场和结尾都非常适合，可是并不适合较高的年级。

下面分别附上几篇简版教案[①]，供参考。

5. IB课程教案

Lesson Plan 5: MYP G6 – Phase 1-2-3 MYP English Language Acquisition

本教案为国际学校IB课程中学英语课教案示例。

---

① 本书绝大多数教案均来自于作者本人的真实教学案例；小学、初中或高中的教案由教师同仁友情提供。在此特别致谢！为避免不必要的误会，对涉及隐私和不必要示范的信息均作了删减修改。教师朋友在评鉴参考之余，可进行升级完善。

Date:	29 April – 3 May
Class:	MYP Year 1 – G6 – Phase 1 – Phase 2 – Phase 3
Subject:	English Language Acquisition
Standard(s) / Learning Outcomes:	**Reading** P1-Reading text of 200–300 words and answer simple questions. P2-Reading text of 400–500 words. Answer questions about main ideas and supporting details. P3-Reading text of 600–700 words. Understand specific information, ideas, opinions and attitudes. **Listening & Speaking** P1-Understand and respond to simple spoken texts P2-Express feelings and opinions P3-Communicate information with relevant ideas and some details in familiar and unfamiliar situations **Writing** P1-Simple phrases and sentences from a limited range of everyday situations. 100–150 words P2-Express feelings and opinions in writing in simple format. 100–150 words P3-Express thoughts, ideas and opinions about topics of personal interest to everyday life. 200–250 words
Unit: 4	The Dangers of Secondhand Smoke
Global Contexts:	Identities and Relationships

Key Concepts:	Perspective – Health and Social Issues related to smoking
ATLs:	Communication and Research
IB Learner Profile	Knowledgeable and Reflective
Timing - Minutes	Activity and resources
15	Brainstorming - Spider Web
30	End of Unit 4 vocabulary review: The Dangers of Secondhand Smoke Spelling – Meaning – Pronunciation – Articles review
Monday 29 April	A practice writing task – Differentiation Write short sentences using words from the taught vocabulary list. Phase 1-three short sentences using words from the vocabulary list Phase 2-five sentences using words from the vocabulary list Phase 3-a short paragraph using words from the vocabulary list
Tuesday 30 April (Double)	Writing task assessment - Criteria C, D A letter to a friend or family member describing the dangers of smoking Phase 1 & Phase 2- 100–150 words; Phase 3- 200–250 words

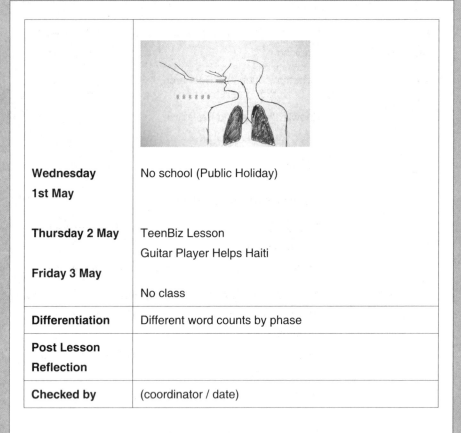

Wednesday 1st May	No school (Public Holiday)
Thursday 2 May **Friday 3 May**	TeenBiz Lesson Guitar Player Helps Haiti No class
Differentiation	Different word counts by phase
Post Lesson Reflection	
Checked by	(coordinator / date)

⑥ 小学英语课程教案

Lesson Plan 6: Then and Now

本教案为小学英语课程教案示例。

学科		班级		时间		教材		授课老师	Fay
课题		人数		时长		出版社		指导老师	Janet

教学目标①	知识目标：了解……等知识。 能力目标：培养学生的阅读能力和综合运用知识的能力；培养用英语交流的习惯，培养良好的语音、语调和语感。 1. 能熟练运用……等句型交流； 2. 能正确听，说，读……等词汇，并用来描述……； 3. 适当拓展相关词汇。 情感目标：培养学生应该尊重每一个人，不能有以貌取人的意识。
教学重点难点	重点：能阅读短文，完成相应练习。 难点：能用过去式描述……。

---

① 21世纪，核心素养概念逐渐在各国受到普遍重视，由此，在各学科教学中，核心素养的培养也自然而然地融进了教学目标中。一般来说，学科核心素养是指通过学习而逐步形成的关键能力、必备品格与价值观念。可参见杨久诠主编的《学生发展核心素养三十人谈》（上海：华东师范大学出版社，2017年3月）和中华人民共和国教育部制定的《普通高中美术课程标准》（2017年版，北京：人民教育出版社，2018年1月）等文献资料。此处教育目标除了英语学科的语言知识和技能目标外，还有核心素养的培养，比如情感目标。

教学过程

Step 1: Warming-up : Sing a song. (*"Look at Me Now"*)

Step 2: Make a Chant.

Step 3: Review Words: ... / Sentences : ...

Step 4: New lesson vocabulary. Words : polite, shy, hard-working, helpful, clever.

Step 5: Bomb Game. (Two rounds)

Step 6: Listen to the new dialogues / sentence patterns:

What's ... like?

He is hard-working / ...

Practise the sentence patterns. (Let students use the sentence patterns one by one.)

Step 7: Group Work: Do a survey.

Ask your group's family members: What's your father / mother / brother like?

He / She is ....

Step 8: Pair Work: Make a dialogue with your partner.

Step 9: Summary.

Words and sentence patterns.

You can't judge a book by its cover.

Step 10: Evaluation.

Which group is the best?

Step 11: Homework.

Make a new dialogue with your partner.

Step 12: Do a finger play.

板书设计	
课后反思	本节课……。学生能积极参与……但是也存在一定的不足。首先，……。以上三个方面在以后的工作中需要提高。

7. 初中英语课程教案

Lesson Plan 7: I'll Help Clean up the City Parks.

本教案为初中英语课程教案示例。

I. 教学目标 Teaching Objectives

Skill Focus		▲ Listen and talk about offering help. ▲ Talk about ways to tell people about the Clean-Up Day. ▲ Listen, describe and talk about the work of the volunteers. ▲ Learn to write a letter. ▲ Learn to deal with new problems or situations using what has been learned.
Language Focus	功能句式	**Talk about offering help** I'd like to work ... You could help by ... **Talk about ways to tell people about the Clean-Up Day** We need to ... We can't ...

Language Focus	功能句式	**Talk about the work the volunteers do** These three students all volunteer their time to help other people. Somebody loves to ... / helps ... / plans to ... / wants to ... I like ... You could ...
	词汇	1. 重点词汇 advertisement, fix, repair, blind, deaf, shut, carry, fetch 2. 认读词汇 hunger, homeless, cheer, clean-up, sign, establish, major, commitment, elementary, veterinarian ... donation, part of speech, pronoun, adverb, preposition, conjunction 3. 词组 clean up, cheer up, give out, put off, set up, think up, take after, fix up, give away, put up, hand out, work out, at once
	语法	How to use phrasal verbs.
Strategy Focus		1. Matching 2. Personalizing 3. Using parts of speech
Culture Focus		Being a volunteer is useful and important.

II. 教材分析和重组 Teaching Materials: Analysing and Rearranging

1. 教材分析

本单元以Volunteering为话题设计了四个部分的内容。

Section A

该部分有四个模块:

第一个模块围绕ways in which you could help people这个话题展开叙述，听力、口语训练;

第二个模块围绕Talk about ways to tell people about the Clean-Up Day进行听力、口语训练;

第三个模块是关于volunteers的一个阅读材料，训练形式为阅读，填表格，角色表演;

第四个模块仍以the kinds of work the volunteers do为话题，开展小组对话活动。

Section B

该部分有四个模块:

第一模块是词汇的学习与运用;

第二模块以听力训练形式强化第一模块中所学词汇和口语训练;

第三模块围绕中心展开阅读a volunteer's work并再次强化了第一模块中的词汇学习;

第四模块仍就the work the volunteers do这一话题以小组活动形式进行口语训练。

Self check

该部分有两个模块：

第一模块对所学词汇进行填空训练；

第二模块以某一志愿者的活动为内容进行写作和口语练习。

Reading

该部分共设四项任务:

第一项任务以问题讨论的形式激活相关的背景知识；

第二项任务要求学生通过快速阅读获取信息，并鼓励学生运用词性的知识阅读和理解短文内容；

第三项任务通过提炼阅读材料中的知识点和难点进一步理解文章；

第四项任务以写回信的形式对所学知识进行巩固运用。

2. 教材重组和课时分配

Period 1: (Section A) New function presenting

Period 2: (Section A) Practise

Period 3: (Section B) Integrating skills

Period 4: (Section 1 – Section 4) Reading

Period 5: (Self check: 1, 2) Self check

III. 分课时教案 Teaching Plans for Each Period

Period 1   New function presenting

语言目标 Language goals	Words & expressions 生词和短语	clean up, hunger, homeless, cheer up, give out, clean-up, sign, put off, set up, establish, major, commitment, veterinarian, coach
	Key sentences 重点句子 (P60)	I'd like to work outside. You could help clean up the city parks.
能力目标 Ability goals	Enable the students to talk about offering help.	
	Enable the students to talk about the Clean-Up Day.	
情感和 态度目标 Emotional & attitudinal goals	Enable the students to form a positive attitude to help others.	
策略目标 Strategy goals	To understand the target language by reading the pictures.	
文化意识 目标 Culture awareness goals	Being a volunteer is great! How to offer help to others.	

教学重点 Teaching important points：

Enable the students to talk about offering help.

教学过程与方式 Teaching procedures and ways：

Step I Lead-in (1a: P60)

T: In the last unit, we learned how to respond if you asked me where you would like to visit.

Ss: Yes. We would also like to visit there because of its beautiful scenery and kind people.

...

Step II Listening (1b: P60)

T: Now let's listen to an audio / video in which some people describe what they want to do as volunteers ...

(Play the tape twice and then check the answers with the whole class.)

Step III Oral Practice (1c: P60)

T: From the listening, we have heard some things volunteers want to do. Please work in pairs and make conversations to express your own opinions.

Sample dialogue 1:

S1: I would like to work outside.

S2: You could help plant trees and grass to beautify our hometown.

Sample dialogue 2:

S1: I'd like to work in the hospital.

S2: Then you could help cheer up the patient.

Sample dialogue 3:

S1: I'd like to work at a station.

S2: You could help the passengers with their luggage.

Step IV Practice (2a, 2b, 2c: P61)

T: Let's listen to another audio in which some students are talking about ways of helping ...

Sample dialogue 1:

S1: We need to hand out advertisements after school.

S2: Let's have supper first.

S1: No, we can't put off handing out the advertisements. Clean-Up Day is only two weeks from now.

Sample dialogue 2:

S1: We need to put up the signs.

S2: Let's drink some water first. I'm thirsty.

S1: No, we can't put off putting up the signs. Clean-Up Day is five days from now.

Sample dialogue 3:

S1: We need to put up a notice.

S2: Let's have supper first.

S1: No, we can't put off putting up the notice. Clean-Up Day is just two days from now.

Step V Summary and Homework

T: In this class, we've mainly talked about offering help. After class, try to make more dialogues to practise. Also learn the phrasal verbs in Grammar Focus: cheer up, set up and come up with. If you cannot fully understand their meanings and usage, please look them up in the dictionary.

8. 高中英语课程教案

Lesson Plan 8: Healthy Eating

本教案为高中英语课程教案示例。

授课教师	Judy	时间	5月	指导教师	Cathriona
授课内容	必修三第二单元 Healthy Eating			共（1）课时第（1）课时	
教材采用	（人民教育）出版社第（3）册第（2）单元第（1）课时				
授课班级		课型	阅读课	班级人数	
学情分析	"健康饮食"是学生感兴趣的话题之一。面对越来越多的食品安全问题，面对越来越多的肥胖问题，学生们有话可说。这篇阅读课文是介绍"饮食习惯"的文章，包括传统饮食习惯的改变，日常饮食选择，旨在让学生明白健康的饮食习惯的养成是拥有健康体魄的前提。				

	本篇文章生词量较大（共有546个单词，其中包括34个生词），标题较抽象，各段主题句分布不太明显（大部分分布在段落中间）。且大部分学生对饮食与健康的关系（如人体每天必须摄入的六种基本营养成分的来源、健康饮食的重要性、什么是绿色食品等）了解较少。因此，本文的学习难度较大。
教学目标	**知识目标：** a）使学生了解protein，calcium等基本营养成分的来源和主要功能，健康的饮食习惯是健康的保证，以及素食主义等信息。 b）学习掌握有关营养成分与食物的词汇，如：protein、calcium、carbohydrate、fibre、mineral、vitamin、vegetarian &energy-giving food, body-building food等，以及be rich in和否定表强调的用法。 **能力目标：** a）使学生学会克服生词障碍，通过略读，寻找文章的主题句，理清文章的总体框架与脉络；通过查读，捕捉文章的重要细节，理解作者的写作意图。 b）使学生学会运用各种猜词技巧，猜测部分生词在具体的语言环境中的含义。 **情感目标：** 使学生学会审视自己、审视食物，提高养成健康饮食习惯的意识。
重点难点	1）让学生认识到饮食对健康的重要影响。 2）侧重培养学生对文章整体结构的把握，突出培养学生以下3个方面的能力： a. 把握文章中心的能力。 b. 根据主题快速捕捉文章重点细节的能力。

	c. 猜词能力。 3）重点掌握有关营养成分与食物的词汇，特别是人体每天必须摄入的六种基本营养成分的词汇以及这些营养成分的来源和主要功能。
教学方法	任务型语言教学法 直观法 合作学习教学法 整体语言教学法
教具	电子白板

教学过程设计（可另附纸）

教学环节	教师活动	学生活动	设计意图
一、导入 （约3分钟）	提问学生： "With the weekend approaching, do you have any plans? For example: We will have a big meal." "What kind of food do you often eat in daily life?"	首先学生们自由发言；老师可在学生发言遇到困难时给予帮助。	以寒暄聊天的口吻自然地引入饮食这个话题，激发学习兴趣。

教学环节	教师活动	学生活动	设计意图
二、热身（约5分钟）	提问学生： "Do you know these fruit and vegetables?" "What are they rich in?" "Do you know that the food you eat helps you to grow in different ways?"	通过PPT提示食物名称、营养成分和句型"I like ... best, for they are rich in ..."来回答问题；然后了解食物的分类，并了解各类食物如何帮助我们的生理机能正常运作。	使学生能在口语操练中使用已学词汇描述自己的朋友，并掌握句型。PPT提示有助于学生表达。
三、课前阅读（约2分钟）	Predict from the title "Come and Eat Here". 1.Where could it happen? 2.Who will be there? 3.What food could be served there?	通过文章标题预测文章内容。	让学生们从标题的关键词中推测文章内容，引起阅读兴趣。并认识到标题的重要性。
四、阅读（约20分钟）	Fast reading: Find out the main idea of the passage. What different places are mentioned（提及）in the text?	略读课文，找出文章的大意；找出文中提到的三个地点 。	采用填空的形式降低难度；训练学生整体把握文章脉络的能力。

教学环节	教师活动	学生活动	设计意图
	Careful reading: Part 1 1. By lunch time, his restaurant was empty, which ought to be full of people. 2. The menu in Wang Peng's restaurant 3. How does he feel? Part 2 1. Fill in the blanks. 2. How does he feel? Part 3 Comparison: his menu versus her menu Structure analysis:	按照地点转换分为三部分后细读每部分，并有针对性地设问，重点把握人物情感。	解读文章每部分的细节，体会人物心情和情感，训练学生捕捉细节的能力。
五、总结 （约5分钟）	Retell the story.	回顾总结文章内容。	检验学生是否掌握理解了文章的内容、结构和发展逻辑，训练总结归纳能力。

教学环节	教师活动	学生活动	设计意图
六、分组讨论（5分钟）	1. What will Wang Peng do to win his customers back? 2. How do you think the story will end? 3. The title "Come and Eat Here" refers to a restaurant where ... 提出"you are what you eat"。	分组讨论王鹏应对竞争的策略；猜测文章结局；讨论文章标题的含义。	这几个开放式问题有利于学生加深对文章的理解，并在整体把握课文内容的基础上进一步升华。

  教案可以说是教学的行动纲领和指南，所以教案设计与制定至关重要。综合来看，备课要备学情，备上课内容，备上课所需的资源（含教室设备、教学软件、电子教案或线上教学资源等），准备课堂活动组织与课堂管理等。也就是后文中论及的备人、备物、备课。

  课堂教学目标也并不单一，除了英语语言课程必有的语言文化知识和语言技能目标（比如对单词、语句的听、说、读、写、译等），还要有核心素质的培养，比如规则意识的建立、情感的表达、时间管理能力、沟通协调能力、组织领导力等等。笔者曾参与某艺术类课程目标的梳理与讨论。这里按照笔者的理解，尝试用下图来表达该课程目标（含核心素养）的培养。

从上述教案可以看出，由于教学对象、教学目标、教学内容、教学资源和手段方法的不同，教案可以是多种多样的。但是我们也会发现，尽管上述教学内容不同，教案的实质和形式并没有多少变化。读者可以参考上述教案或下面的模板进行教学准备。

9. 通用教案参考模板

Lesson Plan 9: Template

本空白教案为教案参考模板，请根据所教授课程、教学目标和要求，进行修改调整。

授课教师		授课时间		指导教师	
授课内容				授课时长	
采用教材					
授课班级		授课类型		班级人数	
学情分析					

教学目标	知识目标：				
	能力目标：				
	情感目标：				
	其他核心素养目标：				

重点难点	
教学方法	

教学过程设计				
教学环节	教师活动	学生活动	所需物品	设计意图
导入（时长）				
热身（时长）				

教学环节	教师活动	学生活动	所需物品	设计意图
课前阅读 / 课堂活动 一 （时长）				
阅读 / 课堂活动 二 （时长）				
总结 / 课堂活动 三 复习巩固 （时长）				
分组讨论 / 总结 / 作业布置 / 送小朋友 （时长）				
板书设计				
教学反思				

教学场景创设

备课远不止是了解学生和准备授课内容，还要做好另一个重要的准备，场景即教室环境的创设。因为，环境就是第三位教师。(*The physical environment is the "third teacher" in the Reggio Emilia philosophy.*[①])

毋庸置疑，环境创设对语言学习至关重要，创设一个真实的语境会让语言的学习效果事半功倍。下面我们就用两例真实的故事来告诉大家，教室环境创设，真的很简单、很有用！

Everyone knows that creating a rich language environment is key to language learning. Language learning occurs best in a stimulating environment. How can I create such a learning environment? This question was frequently asked by young teachers during training programs or when I talked to them. Obviously, creating a stimulating environment has become more important in modern classrooms. Here are our two teaching stories about establishing such an environment. As you can see, it is not difficult to create a rich classroom environment.

[①] https://en.wikipedia.org/wiki/Reggio_Emilia_approach 语出世界著名儿童早期教育体系之一瑞吉欧的创立人马拉古奇（Malaguzzi）。Malaguzzi believed the physical environment to be of fundamental importance to the early childhood program; he referred to it as the "third teacher", alongside adults and other students.

1. 教学场景准备——窗帘的妙用

Story 1 : An Old, Blue, Plastic Shower Curtain

In Beijing the children were studying about life in the deep ocean. To help to focus the children's learning, I used an old, blue, plastic shower curtain covered with colourful fish. I used this to cover the windows. When the sun shone through them, the effect of being under the sea was very real. Various soft, stuffed toys, such as a clown fish (Nemo), a turtle and a dolphin, were hung from the ceiling to continue the theme, while another teacher provided a large, inflatable, killer whale, which was strung with fishing line near the ceiling where young hands could not reach.

This created a very stimulating environment as we read stories of "The Lonely Sea Monster" and researched other creatures that live in the depths of the sea.

2. 课堂环境创设——教室变丛林

Story 2 : Let's Turn Our Barren Classroom into A Wonderful Jungle

You know that creating a rich classroom sometimes needs fabulous ideas, but this is not enough. Teachers also need more minds and even more muscles. Don't worry, it is the right time for our young assistants to contribute.

Children learn best in a rich language environment to which they can relate. It is even better if they have helped to create that environment.

I taught a Grade Seven class in a national Indonesian high school, where the classroom was devoid of anything on the walls. With windows on both sides and a large whiteboard at the front of the room, there was only the back wall available for display purposes. Twenty-five individual desks and chairs had to be set out in five rows of five for the three classes to use.

Since I was teaching a unit about looking at life through different perspectives, with reading stories being written from an animal's viewpoint, I asked the students to each make ten large coloured leaves for homework. I cut strips of green, crepe paper, which I engaged some willing students into helping me to twist. These were put on the back wall together with the leaves and hung from the ceiling to create a jungle effect. We then cut out some large pairs of eyes to peer through the leaves.

New vocabulary words were added to leaves at the front of the room to further cement their learning.

The children were keen to come to their exciting, jungle classroom to continue their English studies.

Creating a rich learning environment with the involvement of students gives them a sense of ownership and partnership in their learning.

小结、反思与练习
Summary, Reflection and Practice

课前准备得越充分，上课就会越自信，越轻松自如。（ *The more prepared you are before class, the more confident you are in the class.* ）即使遇到突发情况，处理时也会镇定从容。学生年龄小，经常很难控制住自己，作为老师，就要多了解学生，包括他们的年龄、情绪、个性、认知发展甚至他们的家庭情况。因此，请做好：

□ 制定并（用检查单）检查教案，进行周密备课 Plan carefully ；

□ 确定清晰的教学目标（并在上课时让学生也清晰他们的学习目标）Set clear goals ；

□ 了解学生学习的情况（含已知和未知）Find out where your students are at (what they know and / or don't know) ；

□ 创设良好的教学环境（好好装点布置，让学生也参与进来）Enrich your teaching environment ；

□ 教学时尽量把听、说、读、写、译等技能结合起来 Try to integrate / incorporate as many of the listening, reading, speaking and writing skills as you can；

□ 把多感（看、听、说、做、感觉等）也充分调动运用起来 Use the senses as gateways into the students' brains. For example: Students should

- See a letter.

- Listen to you speak its sound (s).

- Say it repeatedly.

- Act it out, if possible. (Be creative.)

- Feel the sound through writing it.

□ 利用讲故事、读绘本、绕口令、吟诗、咏唱等多种形式教学 Use stories as often as possible (Contextual learning); reading picture books (Visual clues support understanding); read and learn poems, tongue twisters and songs (Articulation practice, vocabulary and grammar building)；

□ 让学生开动脑筋 Engage the brain；

□ 时间管理（活动要计时）Time your activities (This skill will improve with experience)。

小结 Your summary

1. _____

_____

2. _____

_____

3.

反思 Reflection

1. I am having difficulty with ...

2. I love to ...

3. I am nervous about ...

练习 Practice

1.

2.

3.

教研团队练习 Group Discussion：

1.分组讨论教学准备（Discuss）

2.分组进行案例分享（Share）

3.分组开展讨论应用（Apply）

课 中 篇
Teaching

第二章
有序有料的课堂教学
Teaching and Learning

　　准备上课啦！教案制定了，教学目标、教学内容、教学环节、教学工具、教室布置、教学方式方法等等都了然于心，可谓万事俱备了。但是请千万记住，你不可能把你的英语知识和技能一下子直接倒入学生的脑子里，也不可能挥动魔术棒一下子把每个学生都变成英语高手。当然，你可以通过教学一步步地引导他们，教会他们。

　　不管什么时候，尽快叫出学生的名字，是教师教学大法中的重要法则！与此同时，一定要清晰地告诉学生们教学目标。有目标，方向就一致，师生同心协力的力量绝对超乎想象。

　　Your first job will be to clearly keep in the forefront of your mind what your objectives are for the lesson. This is what gives focus to successful lessons. Also, don't keep this as a secret. Instead, if possible, let your students know what's happening. By clearly stating the lesson goals, you are letting them understand the purpose of the activities. They can also be involved in determining the success criteria for reaching each goal. How can their success be judged? Will they be able to read and write the sounds for a particular letter or digraph? How will they show their learning? This discussion is all part of making learning visible. Students are more likely to experience success and a sense of achievement if they understand where the lesson is going. If they have had a part in deciding how to assess the achievement of the goals, they are more likely to recognize their success and progress in learning.

在课堂教学中，时刻保持清晰的目标非常重要。Of course, some beginning students will still be dependent upon their home language to make sense of the objective. It may be stated using minimal language. Nevertheless, a clearly stated goal should be conveyed simply to enable students to be active learners. Perhaps it could be written on a WALT (We Are Learning To) chart on the board or with younger non-readers the objective could be told to them and repeated throughout the lesson. This focus must be maintained from the beginning to the and.

As you progress through the planned learning experiences, an effective teacher will continually be gauging the students' understanding of the objectives. Why did a child respond in that way? What is the child thinking? Are they really grasping the concept of the letter sound or grammar point, or are they simply going through the motions of the activity? This continual assessment can take place while students are playing a game or identifying matching letters or words. Any activity is an opportunity for assessment and a good teacher does this all the time.

It should not just occur when learners do a written test. That is just one way of finding out what a student knows, but there are so many other ways it can be done and an effective teacher will be finding out and taking mental notes constantly.

所有的教学环节都要有节奏，给学生适量的思考时间。When teaching students another language, it is imperative that a teacher allows her students sufficient thinking time. This allows them time to translate what their teacher is saying back and forth from their first language to the target language. All students will do this until they are competent enough to think in the target language. Some researchers have suggested eight seconds to be the usual wait time for a student to respond to a question. However, in my experience it will vary for each individual; nevertheless, eight seconds is a useful rule of thumb. This often requires teachers to slow down and pause in their own thinking, which can be difficult to do as our minds are extremely active while we are teaching.

少说多教。Another useful way of thinking for a teacher during the course of a lesson is to talk less and teach more. As teachers, we are very prone to talking throughout the entire lesson. We talk to the students and explain absolutely everything, whether they understand or not. However, research has shown that effective teaching allows students to do more of the thinking, so they can reach the conceptual understanding without requiring the teacher to speak through every minute of the lesson. They should be active in making connections to their learning. The teacher can ask pointed questions and give the students opportunities to respond through a drawing or an action, if they can't yet express themselves fully in a sentence.

下面列举几个真实的课堂教学案例。

1. 抓住学生兴趣点——漫画与对话

现在越来越多的学校认同并践行"以学生为中心"的教育理念。从幼儿园开始，我们就激发并培养学生对未知世界的探索兴趣，让他们不断进行自我体验学习。兴趣就是最好的老师，课堂教学一旦以学生为中心，学生在课堂上的表现就会十分活跃，也十分有想法，有时候甚至对老师也是一种很大的挑战。高效能教师能时刻在学生的学习兴趣和教学内容之间做好平衡，抓住学生的兴奋点，随机调整教学方法和策略。

Story 3：Comics and Dialogues

I walked into the fifth-grade classroom as usual one day. I was fully prepared, teaching plan, materials, contents ... everything was kept in my mind. This lesson was to review the food vocabulary and make a personal healthy eating pyramid based on the category of food.

I wrote the teaching objectives on the upper left corner of the whiteboard after a warm-up activity. A Swiss child asked "Madam, can we draw comics?" Before I knew it, she had rushed to the front and had quickly drawn four cartoon characters, each with an oval on the side of the cartoon character's mouth. I suddenly understood what she meant; she wanted to learn sentences by using comic pictures. The other students all agreed by their applause; they were extremely excited. At that very moment, I had a choice. I could continue teaching as planned, but that would lower their spirits and interests, because their attention had been shifted to comics. They still loved learning in a visual way even though they were fifth-grade children. But how could I complete my planned teaching if I followed their desires? How could I achieve the planned objectives for this class? What should I do?

I quickly made a decision with a smile, "No problem. But we must review the basic vocabulary and commands using several dialogue patterns. Otherwise, how could you draw a comic with a conversation?" Everyone applauded and nodded. Promptly I wrote down on the whiteboard how to order – a meal, which is what I planned to teach them. Pair-work was assigned to draw the comics and practise the dialogue within fifteen minutes, and the task would end with their presentations in ten minutes. They could choose to role-play using their comics, or just role-play without any pictures. To save time, most of them chose to role-play, and they performed very well that day.

As you can see from the example above, do not always expect your class to go as you planned, because you are teaching children who are full of wonder and surprise.

2. 迎合好奇心——跳到课桌上的熊孩子

不要总是期待课堂上按部就班，一如你所编写的教案那样循序渐进。

因为，你教授的是一群孩子，他们总是充满了好奇。比如，你遇到了一个在课桌上跳来跳去的熊孩子。

Story 4 : A Boy Dancing on Top of the Desk

I shall never forget the day that a young six-year-old joined my ESL classroom. This student behaved more like a wild animal. He thought that it was fun to jump up on top of the desk. When I asked him to come and join the class on the carpet, he then thought that it was time for a game of tag. He dared me to catch him as he jumped from desk to desk and scampered around the floor.

What was I to do? Chasing after him just fueled his desire to play this game. The other children were watching and a few of them were itching to join in.

If I ignored him, would the other children concentrate on me or on this little circus clown?

I chose to quickly ask all the children to sit in a circle on the carpet and began to read them a story. Within a minute the troublesome new student had lost the desire to play his game and had crept over to listen to the story.

Unfortunately, he then began hugging an unsuspecting student, who reacted against his behaviour. Carefully I had to remove the other student from him while keeping the class occupied with this story.

Surely, there is never a dull moment when teaching young children another language.

3. 应对好动学生的课堂管理——动起来

课堂管理是教师工作的重要环节，也是教师培训中最受欢迎和必不可少的课程。课堂管理的经验需要时间来慢慢打磨积累，但有些方法或注意事项还是可以通过学习和实践迅速掌握。比如故事4中的熊孩子，若是教师不留神，就演变成了互相追逐的游戏，甚至会导致整节课注意力的严重偏失。而高效能教师在遇到这种情形时，会迅速调整教学方式，让学生坐成一圈讲故事，不仅教学秩序井然，连熊孩子也被吸引过来沉浸在学习中。故事5同样如此，教师迅速调整了教学步骤和教学内容，迎合了学生的学习热情，教学效果超乎意料。

遇到一刻不得闲、多动的孩子，你又会怎么"管"呢？Learning how to effectively manage a class full of excited children requires a lot of effort and experience. A few more examples are listed here for your reference.

Story 5 : Keep the Lesson Moving

One young Chinese boy came to my class having no prior experience in learning English. His homeroom class teacher was finding him a handful. It wasn't only that he didn't understand any English, this young child would not settle at anything for more than one minute. He was restless and impulsive throughout the whole day.

In my English class, I found the secret was to keep his attention by giving him and the other students opportunities to move frequently.

I would begin the class with singing a song, perhaps while they stood around a table or sat on the floor. Then we would all move to the calendar chart, where they stood while we changed it to represent the correct day, date and weather. He could assist in doing this. Next we might say the days of the week with a partner clapping chant, before sitting on the floor for a mini-lesson about a particular sound. This learning was consolidated by writing the letter on small whiteboards, which the children moved to collect. After a short practice in writing on whiteboards, they moved to the tables with their books where they practised writing the letter in words with simple drawings. Following this, the children might move their chairs to view an animated e-book story projected onto the screen. The restless student might be given the task to turn off the classroom lights. Finally, we would review the letter with a game in which they had to say the sounds or find the letter in the room.

By constantly building movement into the lesson, this child's need to move was satisfied in a productive way.

4. 建立规矩意识——托尼又跑了

所谓管理，自然要有规矩。既然有规矩，就要执行。孩子们规矩意识的建立、培养和加强也是教学的重要内容。你看，别人家的小朋友在排队，熊孩子托尼又跑了。

Story 6 : Tony Ran Out of the Classroom Again

"Tony!"

"Tony!"

"Line up!"

But Tony ran out of the classroom again.

After school when all the other children were waiting in line preparing to leave the classroom together, Tony ran out to the school gate like a wild horse. It happened several times, so that a few of the other children couldn't help being tempted to fly out of the classroom like Tony.

I decided to stop this.

The rule – "No Running" had been posted on the wall and was highlighted, but Tony soon forgot to follow this rule whenever school was over. I asked the assistant teacher to follow to see where Tony went, and patiently let the rest of the children put away their toys and collect their schoolbags before lining up at the entrance.

We waited for a while until Tony came back, looking quite depressed. He said "Sorry" in a low voice and joined the queue.

As we approached the school gate in a line, I thanked Tony's mother for her cooperation. I had just called her asking for her help to send Tony back when she saw her son coming to the school gate alone, emphasizing how important it was for her child to follow and obey rules, not only in the classroom but also out of it. She agreed with me.

So many children run randomly when school is over, and even some run out of the school. The resulting chaos might cause danger to these children and others; in fact, safety can be lost when young children go out of school amongst cars and buses by themselves.

Rules are rules; everyone must abide by them. The awareness of following rules and regulations symbolizes the advancement of a society. It is also important for children to learn to submit to rules, since this can sometimes be a matter of life and death. When children obey the rules in a classroom, they also tend to follow the other rules out of the classroom.

孩子们在课堂内养成了遵守规矩的意识，他们也就会相应地学会遵守课堂外的规矩。井然有序由此产生。

Some important rules or regulations are recommended to post on the walls around a classroom, so that students can see them clearly. It is better to adhere to the FFC (Fair, Firm, Consistent) principle, which will cause children to respect and follow the rules even if they do not like them. If you are inconsistent and constantly changing the rules, even those who are very young will find the vulnerabilities of your management skills and some will grab the opportunity to make full use of your weaknesses.

课堂管理的最高境界不是"管"，而是通过丰富生动有趣的课堂来教育。管的目的一直服务于教和育。

Many teachers believe that classroom management is to simply rule or govern the class, which is not necessarily true. Classroom management is always to serve your teaching. In a sense, classroom management can be seen as teaching management. I have often witnessed some teachers repeating the rules again and again in order to keep the children quiet and encourage them to participate in some learning activity. It was not wise to chase after the jumping boy, thus fueling his desire to play a game with him. Once you step into the classroom, your teaching has already begun. Keep your focus in mind, endeavoring to make your class so interesting and instructive that the children will follow you, plunging into the sea of learning. The ultimate purpose of classroom management is not to rule over children but to harness their energy and enthusiasm into learning, by teaching with interesting content and approachable pedagogical techniques.

5. 寓教于乐——无桌椅的教室

教育无时无刻不在，教学亦可无所不用。更迭的四季——春夏秋冬，幻变的天气——风霜雨雪，花草树木、虫鸟鱼虾、玩具布偶，均可以成为教学道具和教学内容。但是在没有桌椅的教室里该怎么教学呢？

Story 7 : With No Desks or Chairs

Imagine being shown to a classroom without any desks or chairs on your first day of your professional teaching career by your new principal. That's what happened to me over forty years ago.

The only piece of furniture was an old piano sitting in the corner. Into that empty room just a short time later, I led twenty-four excited six to seven-year-old boys and girls on their first day in Grade Two. What was I to do with them?

I sat the children in a circle on the floor and immediately started getting to know the children through a repetitive chant accompanied with some body percussion. I slapped my knees, clapped my hands and then clicked my fingers once in a pattern. The children copied me. Then I introduced my name and asked them for their names, while keeping the pattern going. "My name is Mrs Vaughan. What is your name?" Each child inserted his / her name into the chant pattern and asked the next child what his / her name was.

Then I made use of the piano to teach the children some songs. These included action songs such as "If you're happy and you know it ..." We composed new words and actions for the songs.

The happy morning continued with reading a picture book from inside my bag and playing other circle games, before our classroom furniture began to arrive.

6. 灵活的教学方式——飞鞋教K

有时候，TPR（全身反应教学法）（详见第三章P110）的效果真的会超出我们的想象。

Story 8 : My Flying Court Shoe

One morning I was energetically teaching my big class of five-year-old children the letter k explaining both its sound and how to write it without using its letter name. I told the young students that this letter was very bad-mannered because he liked to kick things. This is why this letter is usually found at the end of words rather than at the beginning. Turning to the blackboard, I showed the children how to write the letter drawing a large lower-case letter k, which included a shoe at the end of the letter with a ball nearby. Then I turned to the class and said it was "k the kicking k" while dramatically kicking my foot into the air. Suddenly and to my horror, my court shoe flew off my foot into the air. Thankfully it missed landing on any of the now fully attentive children. That was a letter that they never forgot.

I always have taught the alphabet letters by just using the sounds, as I believe the sound is far more important than the letter name when you are learning to read and write. We don't use letter names when we sound out words in reading, nor when we try to spell an unknown word phonetically.

7. 创意教学法——糖果包装设计与取名字

没有桌椅又能如何，发挥你的灵活性和创新能力，你一样可以成为高效能教师。那么，孩子们读完故事、看过影片之后，还应干点什么呢?

Story 9 : Charlie & the Chocolate Factory

The students in my Grade 7 English language class focused their reading and learning on "Charlie and the Chocolate Factory". They read excerpts from this famous novel by Roald Dahl and enjoyed watching some of the movie, "Willy Wonka and the Chocolate Factory", allowing the students to increase their vocabulary and comprehension skills.

As a finale to our studies, I asked the children to design their own special candy wrapper including an original name with a secret candy inside it. They could buy or make their own confectionary, but the wrapper had to be their own work.

These were shared at a special Willy Wonka party during our last lesson with the students reading out their wrappers and explaining why they had chosen the name.

It was all a lot of fun.

8. 应景教学设计——石头汤的故事

教师的教学是一个充满了灵活创意的工作，从课前准备的创意教室环境布置，到创意课堂整体和细节设计，再到考虑创意教学方法，灵活性和创新性无处不在。还有一个非常重要的特征，要应时应景。

As you may see through the above examples, flexibility and creativity see a different, unplanned learning experience that must be taken advantage of before it disappears; rather than being rigidly bound to the planned lesson. The teacher, who resolutely does only what he has planned, will miss wonderful opportunities to engage a student holistically in building vocabulary and expanding their horizons. An effective teacher makes the most of every situation that unexpectedly arises.

Story 10 : I'm Hungry

Just before lunchtime one day, the Grade One children were busily writing a procedural text showing how to make vegetable soup, while it was simmering in the classroom. After reading the traditional folk tale, "Stone Soup", the children had brought in different vegetables. They had washed and cut the vegetables into small pieces, before putting them, together with some stock, into a pot of water to cook. The smell was filling the classroom as the children wrote the instructions.

As I sat at a table helping all the ESL children with their writing, one young Chinese boy who had very limited English began to sing "I'm so hungry". All of the children and I joined in singing this favorite song, which I had taught them a few weeks earlier.

Again, it proved to me the power of music as a vehicle for learning vocabulary. This child had connected and applied that song to this situation, giving him some important vocabulary to articulate his feelings.

I'm Hungry! [1]

I'm so hungry,

so hungry,

so very, very hungry.

I want something I can munch.

I want something I can crunch.

I haven't had my lunch.

I'm hungry!

I'm so hungry,

so hungry,

so very, very hungry.

I'm Hungry!

[1] The composer of "I'm so Hungry" is unknown. It is from "The Useful Book:
Songs and Ideas from Play School". Sydney: ABC Books, 1988.
I learnt this song over 35 years ago, when my own children were very young. Its
catchy tune and repetitive lyrics have made it ideal for children learning English.
Over the years, I created the worksheets to go with it.

9. 课堂游戏活动——小组配对游戏

千万不要说你不喜欢游戏。不管你是否喜欢，学生喜欢。游戏是他们的至爱！谁不愿意玩中学，学中玩呢！Everyone likes games; especially children. Therefore, let us utilize this strategy to maximize our teaching and learning through playing games.

Story 11 : Matching Game

For a couple of years, I had the pleasure of teaching English to first language Indonesian students who were in their first year of secondary school in Jakarta. These twelve to thirteen-year-old students were challenged each week to expand their vocabulary by learning the meanings and spelling of twelve to fifteen set words, which were introduced during their literature study. In order to practise these words, we often played a game matching the meaning to each word.

First, I would prepare a listing of the words along with a definition of each word. Since the twenty-five students were seated in five rows of five desks, I cut out five sets of words and meanings, all on separate small slips of paper. Armed with these five sets, I would place one set on the desk at the head of each row. Each row of students formed a team. Upon the command "Go", the teams of students worked together to match each word with its meaning. The first team to return to their own desks in their row would be deemed to be the winner, if they had also correctly sorted the vocabulary.

> *The competitive nature of the game ensured all the students were actively involved in thinking about the words and thus expanding their knowledge of vocabulary.*

10. 游戏的微创新升级版

游戏在教学中的地位不言而喻。除了不断学习并选择适合的游戏来开展教学外，利用原有的游戏进行一点点的小创新或改进，你也可以收获更多更好用的游戏。故事12是微创新后用于培训的游戏活动。你也可以参考后再做创新。

Game-based learning is an important, useful and practical way of teaching / learning. More examples will be demonstrated in the following pages. There are so many different teaching approaches, but most important of all is to find the one which is yours. And remember: be flexible and creative.

Story 12 : Game X.0

后图是曾经在培训时使用过的游戏1.0版本（Game 1.0）。

The game below is one we used in teacher training. Game 1.0

ZIP 1.0

ZIP 1.0	
Language	Calling out numbers according to given formula
Skills	Listening and speaking
Control	Controlled
Level	Beginner
Time	5-10 minutes
Materials	None

Procedure :

说错的学生淘汰，
胜利组秘籍一封。

Preparation
None

Procedure
Class or group work

The aim of the game is for the learner to count around the class from 1 to 100 without saying a chosen number or a multiple of it. For example, if you and the class choose 4, they must not say 4, 8, 12, 16, etc. Instead of saying these numbers, the player, whose turn it is, must say "ZIP", e.g.

Learner 1: One.
Learner 2: Two.
Learner 3: Three.
Learner 4: ZIP!
Learner 5: Five.
...

我们的要求是请入职接受培训的教师把游戏1.0升级到2.0。

很多教师可以举一反三、触类旁通。他们把ZIP换成了颜色——RED。也有学员教师保留ZIP不变，把数字1、2、3换成了三种颜色，如Red、Yellow、Blue，把学习目标换成了三种颜色，从而把游戏1.0演变成为游戏2.0。

若是由你根据你即将要上的课的教学目标来做微创新，把上文所述的游戏2.0升级为3.0，你打算如何处理呢？实际上，在给学员教师培训时，我们是把培训的每一个环节都通过不同的游戏来实现或呈现的。既然是游戏培训，自始至终都由游戏组成。但请记住，不管如何创新，所有的游戏都是服务于教学目标的，而且要根据学生的实际可接受度来设计制定。Of course, this game always depends on the age of the children and what they already know, as well as what the teaching objectives are.

小结、反思与练习
Summary, Reflection and Practice

灵活、有趣、实用、有效的教学方法有很多，但最重要的是要找到最适合你的。（ *There are so many interesting and flexible ways to teach, but the most important of all is to find the style suitable to you.* ）请记住以下要点：

☐ 有清晰的教学目标和标准（并让你的想法可见）Have clearly stated lesson objectives and success criteria. (Make your thinking visible.)

☐ 课堂管理有章法（公平、严格、一致）Manage the classroom with rules and FFC principle.

☐ 教学有方法有技巧 Use pedagogically sound techniques.

☐ 玩中学 Teach through play.

☐ 灵活创新 Be flexible and creative.

☐ 时刻精准判别学生的掌握程度 Continually gauge students' understanding. (AfL-Assessment for Learning.)

☐ 少说多教 Use less talk for more teaching.

☐ 确保给学生足够的时间（等待他们）并让他们有时间反思 Ensure sufficient wait time and give students time to reflect.

☐ 教师自我反思——不断自我评估 Reflect on the lesson and continually assess your own teaching (AfT).

☐ 对自我适度宽容，给自己成长提升的时间 Be kind to yourself.

问自己以下问题：

* 达到教学目标了么？ Did I achieve my goals?

  ◊ 为什么？ Why / Why not?
* 哪些地方教得好？ What went well?
* 哪些地方还可以再提高？ What could have been improved?
* 后面打算做什么？ Next steps?

小结 Your summary

1. _____

_____

2. _____

_____

3. _____

_____

反思 Reflection

1. My students ...

2. My teaching plan ...

3. The activities ...

练习 Practice

1.

2.

3.

教研团队练习 Group Discussion：

1.分组讨论教学准备（Discuss）

2.分组进行案例分享（Share）

3.分组开展讨论应用（Apply）

第三章
不可不知的教学法
More about Teaching – Methodologies

外语教学理论和方法流派众多，如翻译法（Translation Method）、直接法（the Direct Method）、听说法（the Audio-lingual Approach）、认知法（the Cognitive Approach）、交际法（the Communicative Approach）、沉默法（the Silent Way）、提示法（Suggestopedia）、社区语言学习法（Community Language Learning）、全身反应教学法（the Total Physical Response Method）、沉浸式教学法（the Immersion Approach）、整体教学法（the Whole Language Approach）、基于内容的教学法（the Content-Based Approach）、任务型教学法（Task-Based Language Teaching Approach）、项目式教学法（Project-Based Language Teaching Approach）、探究式教学法（Inquiry-Based Learning）、分层教学法（Differentiated Instruction Strategies）、游戏教学法（Game-Based Learning）、合作式学习教学法（Cooperative Learning Structures）等等。

任何一种流派的理论或教学法都是在一定的历史背景下，以某一种理论作为支撑逐渐发展而成，所以说任何一种外语理论和方法都有一定的科学道理。本章简要介绍好用、有效的几种代表性的教学法。

1. 交际法（The Communicative Approach）

交际法可以说是外语教学法史上的一个里程碑，因为交际法标志着外语教学法告别了以教师为中心的传统的外语教学，开启了研究探讨学生认知规律、培养学生主动交际的外语教学新篇章。

交际法也叫功能法（Functional Approach）或意念法（Notional Approach）。交际法是20世纪70年代根据语言学家海姆斯（Hymes）和韩礼德（Halliday）的理论形成的，在80年代逐渐盛行。随着这一时期社会语言学理论的发展，"交际能力"在外语教学界反响强烈，交际教学法也应运而生。交际法强调以学生为主体，要了解学生的需求（learners' needs），在教学中每一个环节都让学生充分理解、积极参与；课堂教学中交际法经常采用二人对话、三五人成组的小组活动以及全班大讨论等形式，在活动中培养其交际能力。换句话说，就是功能应用的交际法，探讨的是如何把学用合一。虽然不排斥语法，但交际法在使用时也不可能详尽讲解语法，这样学生的语言质量会受影响，因此，交际法比较适合于中级以上外语水平的学生。

The Communicative Approach of teaching a language first became popular in the 1980s, when it was realized that many students who had been learning a language for a number of years found it difficult to hold a conversation in the target language. The emphasis in teaching then switched from developing grammatical skills in reading and writing to oral language development by helping students communicate effectively.

In Japan, Korea and China, native speakers were brought in to universities to build this focus. These teachers encouraged students to interact with one another in the target language using a range of topics. These lessons did not tend to rely on textbooks, but were more open-ended being guided by the students' common interests.

When teaching young children, I have always emphasized the importance of communicating with one another orally by using chants and discussions about picture books. Asking simple repetitive questions sung in a rhythmic chant, while the children are seated in a circle, is an example of using the communicative approach to teaching. These chants could be:

"My name is Mrs Vaughan. What is your name?"

"I like eating bananas. What do you like?"

2. 全身反应教学法TPR（Total Physical Response Method）

全身反应教学法主要是通过让学生反复听教师的指令，学生做动作来学习，学生在行动实践中边做动作边学习词汇与语法结构。这种方法能激发学生的主观能动性，在学中做，在做中学，同时也大大强调了对听的能力的培养。但是对于复杂有难度的语言内容就显示出了局限性，因此这种方法比较适用于初学外语的年幼的小学生。本书中课堂教学和管理的故事案例中均有TPR的影子。

James Asher developed the total physical response (TPR) method as a result of his observation of the language development of young children. It is based on the coordination of language and physical movement. In TPR, instructors give commands to students in the target language with body movements, and students respond with whole-body actions.

In order to best help students to learn effectively, students are encouraged to use physical movements of their body in response to various vocabulary. This increases the sensory input and thus heightens their learning.

As I have always believed that young children should be given opportunity to move frequently within a lesson, I have incorporated some movement aspects into my lessons. It is part of my multi-sensory teaching philosophy.

When students are just beginning to learn English, I have taught them various command verbs such as sit, stand, jump, kick, crawl, walk and stop by getting them to do the action that I say. Then I may select one of the students to say the command for the rest of the students to follow.

Another TPR activity that I have found effective is to teach children to discriminate between long and short vowels. The students stand in a line in the centre of the room, while I stand in front of them with the word "long" held in one outstretched hand and the word "short" held in the other. I then say a word, e.g. cap, and the students must move to the side of the room where "short" has been designated, because cap has a short vowel in it. If I say a long vowel word, they must go to the "long" area. Sometimes we have used other actions to show whether a word has a long or short vowel.

3. 沉浸式教学法（The Immersion Approach）[①]

沉浸式教学法，是讲课时老师只讲所要教授的语言，同时借助直观教具、身体动作帮助学生理解课程内容，让学生沉浸在目标语言里，以期获得耳濡目染的效果。

沉浸式教学法始于20世纪60年代的加拿大。沉浸式教学作为一种崭新、有效的第二语言教学模式，是指用非学习者母语的语言作为直接教学语言的教学模式。它首先出现在加拿大魁北克省的双语教育改革中，由于当地官方语言为法语，而很多以英语为本族语的家长希望学校在帮助他们的孩子学习法语的同时也能提高英语水平，于是加拿大政府着手试验，从幼儿园起便开始用法语上课。由于试行后效果良好，很快就推广开来。随后一些国家也开始使用沉浸式教学法。

沉浸式教学法吸取了语言习得与学习的研究成果，主张加大可理解的语言输入量（comprehensible language input），并使掌握外语深入到各门课程中，是使学生学好外语的根本保证。使用沉浸式教学，对教师的要求很高，需要大批量高水平的双语教师。此外，双语的差异以及使用环境的不同对学习的效果影响也很大。

The immersion approach to language learning has been popular in some schools for many years. A child learns Italian in Australia by attending a school,

---

[①] https://www.teflcorp.com/articles/esl-resources/the-immersion-method-of-teaching-english-as-a-second-514/

in which all of his subjects are taught in the target language. There must be little to no interaction in his home language. Instead, the student is completely surrounded by this new language.

This experience is not unlike how many students who attend an international school from a non-English speaking background have had to learn English. Many of my students in Beijing, came from France, Germany, Korea and Japan with no previous English language instruction. Their parents had accepted well-paying jobs in Beijing and so the children were placed in the school where they were surrounded by only English speaking teachers and classmates. These children often made good progress in learning English.

However, it is important in my view for a student to also maintain their home language as this can enable them to become truly bilingual people, with the ability to use both their home language and English.

4. 任务型教学法TBL（Task-Based Learning）

任务型教学（Task-Based Language Teaching / Learning）又称基于任务的教学法，是指教师通过引导语言学习者在课堂上完成任务来进行的教学。这是20世纪80年代兴起的一种强调"在做中学"（learning by doing）的语言教学方法，是交际教学法的发展，在世界语言教育界引起了人们的广泛关注。近年来，这种"用语言做事"（doing things with the language）的教学理论逐渐引入我国的基础英语课堂教学，是我国外语课程教学改革的一个走向。该理论认为：掌握语言大多是在活动中使用语言的结果，而不是单纯训练语言技能和学习语言知识的结果。在教学活动中，教师应当围绕特定的交际和语言项目，设计出具体的、可操作的任务，学生通过表达、沟通、交涉、解释、询问等各种语言活动形式来完成任务，以达到学习和掌握语言的目的。

任务型教学法是吸收了以往多种教学法的优点而形成的，它和其他的教学法并不排斥。任务型教学法具备以下诸多优点：第一，该教学法能够完成多种多样的任务活动，并有助于激发学生的学习兴趣；第二，在完成任务的过程中，将语言知识和语言技能结合起来，有助于培养学生综合的语言运用能力；第三，促进学生积极参与语言交流活动，启发想象力和创造性思维，有利于发挥学生的主体性作用；第四，在任务型教学中有大量的小组或双人活动，每个人都有自己的任务要完成，可以更好地面向全体学生进行教学；第五，活动内容涉及面广，信息量大，有助于拓宽学生的知识面；第六，在活动中学习知识，培养人际交往、思考、决策和应变能力，有利于学生的全面发展；第七，在任务型教学活动中，在教师的启发下，每个学生都有独立思考、积极参与的机会，易于保持学习的积极性，养成良好的学习习惯，帮助学生获得终身学习的能力。由于任务型教学法的开放性，它能吸收其他多种教学法的所长，在英语教学实践和研究中占据着重要的地位。

Task-based language teaching stresses the importance of using meaningful or authentic tasks to facilitate the teaching of English. It is a type of communicative approach to learning a language where the teaching of a grammar point is secondary to accomplishing the task. For this approach to be successful, students should be taught the vocabulary and grammar constructions that they may need to facilitate meaningful communication before they commence the set task.

This student-centred approach can include such things as interviewing another student or teacher about their views on a subject, making a class mural, planning a trip together to a student-chosen destination or planting a garden.

While I don't use this approach as my sole means of teaching, I have certainly tried to engage the students in many authentic tasks. For example, together the students have drawn and painted a classroom mural, before labelling various things in it and adding captions near them. We have also planted seeds and watched them grow, measuring them and writing stories about them. This task began with a discussion about whether particular seeds were living or non-living, dead or alive.

Two days later, the seeds had sprouted or germinated. They had tiny leaves and were growing.
They are alive.

5. 项目式教学法PBL（Project-Based Learning）

顾名思义，项目式教学法是基于项目的教学法的简称，即学生通过一段时间内对某个真实的、复杂的、有挑战性的问题进行调查分析探究，并从中获取知识和技能的教学方法。基于项目的教学法与前述任务型教学法有很多相同之处，这里不再一一赘述，此处强调项目式教学法的几个特点。

其一，项目式教学法注重知行合一，即把所学知识和技能相结合，尤其关注学生的思辨能力、解决问题的能力、团队协作能力和自我管理能力。包含了备受关注的未来领导力的培养。其二，"真实复杂有挑战性"要求该项目与学生生活实际相关联，而且又不能简单，但也防止过于复杂让学生望而却步。其三，因为是项目，其中包含多个任务，既有分工又有协作，时间跨度也因项目而异。需要学生们在一段时间通力合作共同完成。其四，因为时间有跨度、问题有挑战性，教师要全程跟踪，与学生一起反思项目实施中遇到的问题和不断完善或优化解决方案。其五，项目最终成果化展示。

Another communicative and student-centred approach to language learning is to encourage and facilitate students in doing projects. Through preparing and doing these projects students need to communicate as they search for information, exchange ideas and opinions with others before presenting their findings to an audience.

Grade 5 international school students, who are doing the PYP (Primary Years Programme within the IB framework) have to complete an exhibition, which involves selecting a topic of interest, researching it and taking action before exhibiting their findings in a public forum. Students often work in small groups to complete their project over a period of six weeks.

I have guided a few groups of students through their exhibition, asking them questions to clarify their thinking, suggesting avenues for research and helping them to proof-read their exhibition. A group of three boys came from different countries with different home languages, but together they researched how plastic pollution is affecting our oceans.

A Swedish girl and her Filipino friend worked together using their common language of English to research into how singing is good for your health and how it influences people around the world.

6. 差异化教学法（Differentiated Instruction Strategies）[①]

差异化教学法又名分层教学法，是通过多种教学方法教会不同的学生

---

① Char Forsten, Jim Grant, Betty Hollas. *Differentiated Instruction: Different Strategies for Different Learners* [M]. Crystal Springs Books. 2002.

相同或不同的教学内容。差异化教学法通过为不同的学生提供满足其个体需求的任务来确保所有的学生能够参与到教学活动中。这是一种在学生智力因素或非智力因素存在明显差异的情况下，教师仍然有针对性地实施个体化的分层教学，从而达到教学目标的教学方法。

A good teacher has always tried to differentiate her instruction to ensure all students are able to be successful. This type of instruction was common 100 years ago in small one-teacher schools with students of different ages all grouped together in one classroom.

When there are students with differing levels of English language proficiency within one class, it is essential to differentiate lessons so all students are actively involved in learning.

This was the case in the lessons below. Three new students with very little English language had joined my class. The other students were already at an intermediate stage of proficiency; so, my challenge was to keep those students progressing while catering to the needs of beginner students.

Fortunately, I had the assistance of a teacher aide, Ms Mabel, who was able to supervise one group while I worked with the other. She was able to listen to the students read while others worked on learning their single letter sounds using a video I had previously made. They also could use a web-based program to further develop their phonics skills, while I did some grammar work on past tense with the more advanced students.

On Tuesday, Ms Mabel supervised the more advanced students as they searched for words making the /air/ sound, while I taught single letters to the beginner group. Some time, however, was set aside each day for reading a story which was full of visual clues and making it into a story map with the whole group. In this way, the students could develop a shared learning.

表5是Janienne老师和她的助教Ms Mabel一周分层教学的计划表。从表中可以看出，不同学生不一样的教学目标，还有不同的教学内容和教学活动。实行分层教学的教师若是没有助教，在制定分层教学计划时，同样要针对不同的教学对象，设定特别的教学目标、教学内容和教学活动。

表5 一周分层教学的计划表
Table 5: A Differentiated Lesson Sample

Grade 2 Where We Are In Place & Time (Ancient Civilizations)

Week 28   1st–5th April

	Monday Period 5 （12:45 – 1:35）	Tuesday Period 1 （8:00 – 9:00）	Wednesday Period 3 （10:10 – 11:00）	Thursday Period 3 （10:10 – 11:00）
Objectives	1. to speak in sentences 2. to learn alphabet sounds 3. to write using past tense verbs correctly 4. to listen with understanding	1.to read & spell /air/ & /-are/ words 2. to identify verb tenses 3. to comprehend a story 4. to retell main events in a story	1. to analyse sounds in words 2. to listen with understanding 3. to write sentences in past tense 4. to speak clearly	1. to match sounds to letters 2. to use past tense correctly 3. to edit their writing
Activities	Welcome Kejiro (G2.2) & Evan Kim (G2.1). Introduce each other.	Anne, Kejiro & Evan read with Ms Mabel.	Anne, Kejiro & Evan read with Ms Mabel.	Test Anne, Kejiro and Evan on single letter sounds.

	Monday Period 5 (12:45 – 1:35)	Tuesday Period 1 (8:00 – 9:00)	Wednesday Period 3 (10:10 – 11:00)	Thursday Period 3 (10:10 – 11:00)
Activities	Anne, Kejiro and Evan sort alphabet letters with Ms Mabel. Then she reads with them while the other two listen to single letter sounds using my video. Play a grammar game using past tense. Sing the song: "I write, you write, we are ..." Write some past tense and past continuous sentences. Discuss & analyse the word "where". Look at a terracotta warrior. Describe it and list keywords. What could we learn about an ancient civilization from this artifact? Look through China to find a picture of the terracotta warriors. (page 16) Write sentences about it using past tense.	Sing: "I write, you write, we are ..." Play a past tense game. Past Simple Verbs to be Discuss how we can write words with the sound /air/. Teach -are and air. Find and list words with each spelling. (Ms Mabel supervises this.) I teach Anne, Kejiro & Evan the single letter sounds and writing CVC words on whiteboards. Begin to read "Li Fu's Great Aim" by Karen Wallace and make story maps of it using 8 square comic strip box.	Play team games with the class writing words on whiteboards. CVC words and words using "air" and -are sounds, along with digraphs. Continue to read "Li Fu's Great Aim" and make story maps of it using 8 square comic strip box. Brainstorm together what they have learnt about the ancient Chinese civilization.	Kevin, Yuma and Jiahna can work on their story maps of "Li Fu's Great Aim". Continue to read the book together and do two more boxes in their comic strips. Does their comic strip story make sense?
Plenary	What AtLs have we used today? What have they learnt?	Which AtL did they use?	Reflect on what they have learnt today. Which AtL did they use?	Can they add more things to their learning about the ancient Chinese civilization?

	Monday Period 5 （12:45 – 1:35）	Tuesday Period 1 （8:00 – 9:00）	Wednesday Period 3 （10:10 – 11:00）	Thursday Period 3 （10:10 – 11:00）
Observations/Feed-forward			Next week: Grammar exercises Past Simple Verbs to be	

7. 探究式教学法（Inquiry-Based Learning）

探究是IB国际文凭课程教学最为看重的教学方法，可谓是教学原则之首。探究式教学法是典型的做中学（Learning by doing）教学法，在教学中极其常用。该教学法又称发现法和研究法，是教师通过启发式问题引导学生通过阅读、观察、实验、思考、讨论等途径主动探究，自行发现并掌握知识和技能的一种方法。探究式教学法由教师引导，以学生为主体，以学生为中心，启发激励学生发挥主观能动性积极自觉探究世界，发现问题并尝试解决问题。探究式教学法要求教师在教学过程中有较高的循循善诱的引导能力（teacher-guided inquiry），之后就是学生自我驱动的探究（student-driven inquiry）。

探究式教学法由以下几个步骤组成：

Step 1　Introduction: Hook the students' interest by asking them well-prepared questions.

Step 2　Hypothesis: Activating their prior knowledge might be useful.

Step 3　Planning.

Step 4　Research / Exploration / Investigation.

Step 5   Analysis / Discussion / Reflection.

Step 6   Present and share their findings (pair-group-class) and take time to reflect.

举个例子：如何区分Eggs and Seeds？（*What's the difference?*）

教师首先抛出问题吸引学生兴趣，之后让学生想想，用什么样的方法来验证。学生的方法可能如下：

Experimental ideas:

A. Plant them.

B. Heat them.

C. Break them.

D. Weigh them.

E. Put them into water.

学生用自己想出来的方法实验，然后讨论分析，得出结论，最后呈现他们的发现结果。

第一章中的教案1 "*I like jelly*" 就是一堂科学探究课的示范。

Inquiry learning is a form of active learning which poses questions and encourages students to find the answers for themselves, rather than the teacher presenting facts.

I have used inquiry-based learning frequently in my language teaching as I try to get students to inquire into what is the purpose of silent "e" at the end of words. Initially I have set them the task of finding words ending in silent "e" and writing them on post-it notes. Then we have sorted them, checking to see if they really have silent "e" at the end. For example, the word "me" does not have silent "e" because the letter "e" is making a sound.

Through guided discussion, the children wonder what job silent "e" is doing when they study words such as "cap" and "cape", "kit" and "kite", "not" and "note", etc.

They also see if there is something similar happening in the words "like", "made" and "tube".

After establishing the first job of silent "e" in making the other vowel say its name, I then pose them with the question of what silent "e" is doing in words like "little", "apple" and "uncle". I often select words from the ones that they had written on post-it notes.

This inquiry-based learning about silent "e" can take a couple weeks to complete.

I have also encouraged students to inquire into how many ways the "er" sound can be written in English, the results of which were made into a poster as more discoveries were made. This is an inquiry for more advanced learners.

Kath Murdoch's Inquiry Cycle[①] is frequently and widely used in inquiry teaching throughout Australia and the IB Primary Years Programme schools across the world.

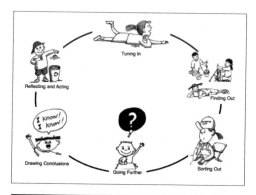

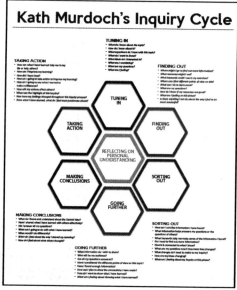

① https://makinggoodhumans.wordpress.com/2015/05/14/inquiry-cycle-why-what-and-how/.
Kath Murdoch. The Power of Inquiry [M]. Seastar Education. 2015.

8. 游戏教学法（Game-Based Learning）

游戏教学法，就是以游戏的形式来开展教学从而达到教学目标的一种教学方法。游戏教学是典型的玩中学，学中玩，寓教于乐，非常受孩子们喜欢，因此也是少儿英语教学中必不可少的教学方法。需要特别注意的是，游戏教学法并不只是单纯的玩游戏，游戏的内容和形式都是服务于教学目标的。比如，第一章"故事改编教案"中字母混合成词、词混合成句、句子混合成故事的游戏，以及第二章"课堂游戏活动——小组配对游戏"，都是利用游戏快乐地完成教学目标的案例。游戏教学法可使用的游戏有很多，教师可以拿来直接使用，或者略作调整创新。

Throughout my years of teaching English in China, I have creatively tried to incorporate children's different strengths and learning styles to help them to remember spelling words.

游戏一：Jumping and Spelling

Some children have practised spelling words aloud while jumping on a trampoline. They would say a word and then the letters, coordinating each letter with a jump. In a school situation the children were supervised by either myself, a teacher aide or a volunteer parent to ensure their safety. This adult would have each word written on a card or a small whiteboard. After reading and spelling the word a couple of times, the visual prompt was removed so that the child would then continue to spell the word a few more times from memory. When the required number of words had been practised in this way, the child would climb off the trampoline and then be asked to write each word as a review.

Repeating this activity every day certainly helped some children to remember their spelling. If no trampoline is available, perhaps just jumping, skipping or doing exercises could be almost as effective, although not quite as much fun.

游戏二：Singing

For children who are musically inclined, I have asked them to make up a song with their spelling words. They could put the spelling word into a well-known song. I have used the famous tune of the Mexican Hat Dance for children to practise words like "anybody" (Say the letter names A-NY-BODY to the tune).

Another example is teaching the tricky word "people" to a jazzy version of the first two lines of "Twinkle Twinkle Little Star".

P-EO-PLE

This is the way we spell people.

A good challenge is for children to make up their own songs for the spelling words. Perhaps successful children could be asked to teach their spelling songs to the rest of the class.

游戏三：Rainbow Writing

Simply writing the spelling words many times is a time-honoured way of learning spelling; but this could be varied by asking the children to write over the top of the same word with a different coloured pen or pencil. Another variation is to make a poster with the word written many different times in different colours and in different styles. Children who are artistic, have tended to enjoy doing this.

游戏四 : Chinese Calligraphy Brush Writing

Many years ago, I purchased five foam brushes used for Chinese Calligraphy on pavements from the HongQiao Pearl Market in Beijing. These brushes have been used many times by students to practise writing their spelling words on the school ball courts.

This kinesthetic approach also appeals to the visual learners.

9. 合作式学习教学法（Cooperative Learning）

众所周知，语言学习需要一定的语言环境，而语境的产生必然要求合作。在合作学习中，同伴间互相协作，不仅共同创造了语境，还在合作中锻炼了合作学习所需的各项技能。

20世纪70年代美国著名教育家David Koonts首先倡导并实施合作式学习。合作式学习尤指课堂教学中的小组合作学习，就是在传统的课堂教学中，借助小组的基本形式，通过小组同伴的沟通与交流，以小组目标达成为标准，以小组总体成绩为评价、奖励依据的教学策略。

美国明尼苏达大学合作式学习中心的约翰逊兄弟（D. W. & R. T. Johnson）也是合作式学习的主要代表人物，他们认为"合作式学习就是在教学上运用小组，使学生共同活动以最大程度地促进他们自己以及他人的学习"。简言之，合作式学习就是学生共同学习，以完成共同的目标。（*In brief, cooperative learning is working together to accomplish shared learning goals.*)

　　本书强调的是合作式学习教学法的重要践行者卡根（Spencer Kagan）博士提出的合作式学习教学法CLS（Cooperative Learning Structures）。[①]卡根博士2009年出版了*Kagan Cooperative Learning*一书，提出了合作式学习的四大原则PIES：①积极互赖（Positive Interdependence）；②人人尽责（Individual Accountability）；③均同参与（Equal Participation）；④同时互动（Simultaneous Interaction）。同时还提出了深受师生欢迎的各种合作式学习方法，这里仅举几例。

① 测试换卡 Quiz-Quiz-Trade

　　第一步：每个学生手里拿着一张卡片（或纸张），站起来（stand up）举起一只手（hand up）并在教室里随意走动，找到另一个正在举手寻找伙伴的同学，二人拍手（pair up）成为一组。

Quiz-Quiz-Trade

Students quiz a partner, get quizzed by a partner, and then trade cards to repeat the process with a new partner.

Setup: The teacher prepares a set of question cards for the class, or each student creates a question card.

---

① Spencer Kagan & Miguel Kagan. *Kagan Cooperative Learning* [M]. San Clemente: Kagan Publishing. 2009.

① The teacher tells students to "Stand up, put a hand up, and pair up."

② Student A quizzes B.

③ Student B answers.

④ Student A praises or coaches.

⑤ Students switch roles.

⑥ Students trade cards and thank each other.

⑦ Repeat steps 1-6 a number of times.

　　第二步：学生A和学生B各自阅读自己卡片上的问题，然后相互回答。回答正确互相鼓励；回答不正确或不完整，互相帮助。在具体实施中，我有时会要求每位同学在卡片背后写上答案，或者提示答案的关键词。

　　第三步：学生A和学生B互相问答后，交换他们的卡片，然后分头举手去找另一位正在寻找伙伴的同学（重复第一步），找到后重复第二步，进而重复第三步，以此往复。问答内容和时长根据教学目标和教学计划而定。

　　卡根博士的合作式学习教学法中同样也有个方法叫作拍手分享（StandUp-HandUp-PairUp），该方法可以用于口头问答（无需卡片）。

② 选卡问答 Fan-and-Pick

　　学生A把写有问题的卡片一字排开，说"请选任何一张卡！"学生B选一张卡片然后大声读出卡上的问题，并给出五秒的思考时间；学生C回答问题；不管正确与否，学生D用自己的话或表扬或完善刚才的回答。对

于无所谓正确与否的答案，学生D无需检查答案的正确性，应直接赞赏并
用自己的话重新诠释答案。然后按顺时针方向转换角色轮流进行上述活动。

Fan-N-Pick

Teammates play a card game to respond to questions. Roles rotate with each new question.

Setup: Each team receive a set of question cards.

① Student A holds question cards in a fan and says, "Pick a card, any card!"

② Student B picks a card, reads the question aloud, and allows five seconds of think time.

③ Student C answers the question.

④ Student D responds to the question:

 • For right / wrong answers, Student D checks and then either praises or tutors.

 • For questions that have no right / wrong answer, Student D does not check for correctness, but praises and then paraphrases the answer.

⑤ Students rotate roles, one person clockwise for each new round.

Modifications: Fan-N-Pick can be played in pairs. Student A fans; Student B picks and reads; Student A answers; Student B tutors or praises; students switch roles.

③ 记录想法 Jot Thoughts

提前准备些剪好的纸条。第一步，教师说出一个题目，规定好思考时间和完成时间；第二步，学生们在每张纸条上写出并宣布一个答案，越多越好；第三步，把每一张带有答案的纸条铺在桌子中间。学生们齐心协力争取用带有答案的纸条把桌子铺满。

Jot Thoughts

Teammates "cover the table," writing ideas on slips of paper.

Setup: Students each have multiple slips of paper (e.g. pre-cut sticky notes, cut-up bond paper).

① Teacher names a topic, sets a time limit, and provides think time (e.g. In three minutes, how many answers can you write down for the question: What are the ways we could reduce poverty?)

② Students write and announce as many ideas as they can in the allotted time, One idea per slip of paper.

③ Each slip of paper is placed in the center of the table; students attempt to "cover the table". (No slip is to overlap.)

④ 互为我师 Rally Coach

第一步，学生A解答问题；第二步，学生B看、听、检查，然后表达赞赏或是给予辅导；第三步，学生B解答问题；第四步，学生A看、听、检查，然后表达赞赏或是给予辅导；第五步，学生A解答问题（即重复第一步）；第六步，学生B看、听、检查，然后表达赞赏或是给予辅导（即重复第二步）。以此反复。

Rally Coach

Partners take turns, one solving a problem while the other coaches.

Setup: Each pair needs one set of high-consensus problems and one pencil.

① Student A solves the first problem.

② Student B watches and listens, checks, coaches if necessary, and praises.

③ Student B solves the next problem.

④ Student A watches and listens, checks, coaches if necessary, and praises.

⑤ Students repeat taking turns solving successive problems.

Note: Rally Coach may be used with worksheet problems, oral problems provided by the teacher, and with manipulatives.

Variation

Pairs Check: After solving two problems, pairs check their answers with the other pair in their team.

卡根博士合作式学习方法还有很多，诸如集思广益（Numbered Heads Together）、圈里圈外（Inside-Outside Circle）等等都十分常用，这里不再一一列举，感兴趣的教师可以仔细研读卡根博士的书籍。

卡根博士的合作式学习教学法之所以风靡世界，是因为这种教学方法一改传统课堂学生参与度极低的弊病，大大提升了课堂教学效果。卡根博士的合作式学习教学法实现了积极互赖（Positive Interdependence）、人人尽责（Individual Accountability）、均同参与（Equal Participation）、同时互动（Simultaneous Interaction），不仅可以应用于教学活动中，甚至可以应用于聚会等其他团体活动中。

小结、反思与练习
Summary, Reflection and Practice

　　教学有则，教学亦有法。而法无定法是指不拘束于某一种法。若加以仔细研读，你就会发现很多教学法是相互交织在一起的。也就是所谓的大道相通。(*Many of these approaches or techniques have common elements; in other words, they are interrelated and interwoven. For this chapter, several approaches, methods, strategies, ways and techniques have been introduced for your reference and information needs.*)

☐ 交际法 The Communicative Approach

☐ 全身反应教学法 Total Physical Response Method, TPR

☐ 沉浸式教学法 The Immersion Approach

☐ 任务型教学法 Task-Based Learning, TBL

☐ 项目式教学法 Project-Based Learning, PBL

☐ 差异化教学法 Differentiated Instruction Strategies

☐ 探究式教学法 Inquiry-Based Learning

☐ 游戏教学法 Game-Based Learning

☐ 合作学习教学法 Cooperative Learning

小结 Your summary

1.

2.

3.

反思 Reflection

1. My class is ...

2. Something that really works is ...

3. I need help ...

练习 Practice

1.

2.

3.

教研团队练习 Group Discussion：

1.分组讨论教学准备（Discuss）

2.分组进行案例分享（Share）

3.分组开展讨论应用（Apply）

地道、标准的教学用语
More about Teaching – Teacher Talk

　　教师的教学用语简洁、明了、到位，对教学效果有至关重要的作用。无论是在日常教师培训时还是在新教师的培训中，教师教学用语都是重要的培训内容。教师本人亦应十分重视使用标准地道的课堂用语。

1. 自我介绍与问候 Self – Introduction & Greetings

Let me introduce myself.
My name is Mrs. Janienne Vaughan. You may call me Mrs. Janienne.
I'll be teaching you English for this semester.
Do you have questions about me?
Please introduce yourselves. It's time for you to introduce yourselves.
Who would like to start first?
Just say "Hi!" or "Hello!" and say your name, like this, "Hello, I'm Andrew. It's nice to meet you."

Please introduce yourselves in pairs.
Please introduce yourselves to your group members.
I'm glad to meet you. Nice to meet you all. It's my pleasure to meet you, students / boys and girls. It's really good to see you again.
Hello, everybody / everyone. Hi, (Jia Xin). (Always add a person's name.)
Good morning everybody. (Only use this before 12 o'clock / noon). Good afternoon, ... (Only use this after 12 o'clock / noon).
How are you? How are you today? How are you this morning / this afternoon?
Very well, thank you. Well, thanks. I'm fine; thanks.
I couldn't be better. Thank you.
Things are fine. Thanks.
Nothing special. Thank you.
Not bad. / So so. / OK. Thanks.
How are you feeling today?
Thank you, I feel wonderful today.
Did you have a good weekend?
I hope you all had a nice weekend.
I'm so glad to see you all.
Did you enjoy your lunch?

What was on today's lunch menu?
I like your jacket today, Jack.
Hi, Andrew, did you have your hair cut? You really look great today.
I hope you'll have a wonderful time here in this school.

2. 取英文名 English Names

Do you all have English names? Have you got an English name? What's your English name?
Don't worry; you'll get one. Who gave you that English name?
Let's all make English names today.
Let's think of some English names for ourselves.
There's a list of English names in this handout.
You've chosen a lovely name. That name suits you.
Qiqi has already chosen "Maggie". Would you like to pick another one?
Names have meanings. Does anybody know what their name means?
The name Sophia means wisdom.
The name Andrew means manly.
Which name is short for Christopher?
Write your English name on this name tag.
Now, let's say our English names in turn.
We'd like to use English names in our class. If you prefer to use your Chinese name, please do so.

前文说过，记住学生名字是高效能教师必修的不二法门。记住学生名字太重要了。可是，给学生取名字千万不可随意，这里面有好多学问。

Story 13 : "Funny" Names

A friend runs a training center for young children to learn English. She asked me for help to take a few classes when a foreign teacher had to leave.

I was really shocked and dazzled the moment I saw the children's English names on the class list. They included names such as Monkey (a girl), Lucky (another girl), Candy (a boy) and Leaf (a girl).

Quick-witted as I was, I briefly explained that names have meanings when I introduced myself. A similar situation happened during the training of young English teachers. I was astonished at the names the young ladies, who were born in the 1990s, had named themselves. At that moment, I even thought I was out of date, because these new chic young ladies were naming themselves deliberately showing off their knowledge, vanity and vogue. However, I was wrong; they knew nothing about the meaning of their names.

Nowadays, many children even some young men and women may believe it is fashionable or necessary to give themselves English names. But, as we know, names are culturally connoted, which means you can never ignore the cultural meaning while naming yourself in Chinese, English or in other language. Take the name, Lucky for example. It is usually used for cats, dogs or other pets. Candy is not suitable for a boy. It's a girl's name. Some people even take bizarre names like Volcano, Vampire and Whipper. Please, do some research before you name yourself like that. Some names like Cherry and Dick are no longer appropriate because they have some (new) meanings which are not acceptable in polite society.

So, what are the taboos for English names? First of all, the names of characters from history, tragedies or disasters are not acceptable. These include Hannibal, Mussolini, Hitler, Jesus or Judas. Secondly, names with "sexual" meanings or implications such as Dick, Cherry and the like, should be avoided. Thirdly, names of fruits and sweets have to be considered cautiously.

Similarly, names of animals and plants such as dragon, monkey, snake and tree, should also be used carefully. Finally, be cautious when choosing names from other cultures.

In fact, with globalization more and more foreign friends like to use Chinese names. In this way, not only do foreigners show their respect towards the Chinese culture, but the Chinese people culturally identify themselves.

In a word, it is important to pay proper attention to the cultural connotations whenever you name yourself or others.

The following names are suitable for your consideration.

Boy's Name	Girl's Name
Andrew / Andy	Lily
John	Sally
Peter	Emma
Jamie / James	Ruby

Boy's Name	Girl's Name
Paul	Anna / Hannah
David	Emily
Noah	Zoe
Leo / Leonard	Jenny
Michael / Mike	Sophie
Micah	Ivy
Joe / Joseph	Ellie
Tony	Kylie

3. 学校和课程 School and Curriculum

Our school is one of the best schools in the city, famous for its quality of English teaching.
This is an English course suitable for beginners / fourth graders.
Let's have a look at the curriculum.
We'll have two lessons a week.
We'll have group presentations once a month and a final exam in June.
At the end of each lesson, you'll take a quiz.
Your class performance will also be assessed.
We'll also have a portfolio for each of you. And you may take it home once every month.
This is our textbook which we are going to use this semester. It has a lot of interesting stories. You may also find a lot of pictures in it. It is an excellent book.

You'll need this workbook for your homework.
Be sure to write your name on the book so that you know it's your book.

4. 班级管理 Classroom Management – Seating & Voting

Please sit in numerical order. Please sit in order of height.
Sit wherever you like. Sit like this every time.
Let's sit in a circle.
Please move your desks and chairs this way.
Please straighten the desks.
Put your desks back to where they were.
Let's draw lots to decide your partners.
Are you all satisfied with your seats?
If you have a problem with your chair or desk, put your hand up.
Let's elect a class president / captain.
The class president represents all the students in our class.
We need a person who has strong sense of responsibility.
We need a chief for our English class.
We need some candidates.
Please recommend some students to become the president.
Jan has recommended Tina to become the president.

Let me nominate some other candidates.
Those who have been nominated, please come to the front.
Briefly make a speech before the election, telling why we should vote for you.
Let's vote.
You have to choose only one candidate.
The one who gets the most votes becomes the class president.
Let's count the votes.
Wow, Jan got 25 votes all together.
Everybody, let's congratulate Jan.
Let's give her a big round of applause.
Let's give a warm welcome to our new class president.
Would you like to say thanks to your classmates?

5. 课堂纪律 Classroom Management – Agreement & Rules

We will make some rules for our classroom and decide the consequences or punishments for breaking them, too.
We need some rules for our classroom.
Please do keep to the rules you have made yourselves.
Let's read the classroom rules together in a loud voice.
I'll post our classroom rules on the bulletin board.
If you break the rules, you will get punished.
First, don't be late for class.

Please be seated when the bell rings.
Don't chat in class.
Never use cell phones in class.
Don't move around during the lesson.
Put up or raise your hands if you have a question.
Don't interrupt when another person is talking.
Never forget to do your homework.
No Chinese; English only in the classroom.
Raise your hand and ask for permission if you want to go to the bathroom.
Never fight.
Use polite language.
Don't lie.
Always respect others.
Be quiet when teachers talk.
Follow the teacher's directions immediately.
Be quiet in the hallway.
Don't spit on the floor.
Don't throw rubbish anywhere.
Don't scribble on your desks.
Always keep the classroom clean.
You'll get a warning if you don't follow the rules.
With three warnings, you'll have to clean the classroom.
Be responsible for your behavior.

Let's check the attendance.
Who's absent today?
Does anyone know why Jan isn't here today?
If you have to miss the class, please call me in advance. / please let me know.
Why did you miss the last lesson / class?
Do you feel better now?
It's good to have you back in class again.

6. 课堂指令 Classroom Teaching – Instructions

Stand up.
Sit down / Take your seat.
Everybody, listen.
Look at me. / Look at this.
Point to the word, ... Point to something that is (red).
Read the next page. Read with me. Let's read this together.
Line up here, please. Please line up at the door. Line up / queue up, now.
Don't cut into the queue. Don't jump the queue.
Find a partner. Get with a partner.

Come here.
Go there. Go outside. Go to the (toilet, playground).
Freeze. (This is said, when you want everyone to stop doing something and not move.)
Stop.
Get a pencil. Get an eraser. Pick up your book. Collect your things.
Sit in a circle. Sit in a semi-circle.
Follow me.
Open your book to the next page. Open your book to page (12). Look at page ....
Close your books. Put your things away.
What is this?
Who has (a blue balloon)?
Put them here. / Put them there.
Hands up.
Hold up your right hand. Hold up your left hand.
Collect your books. Get your books.

Calm down.
Be quiet!
Lower your voice.
Use indoor voice.
Wait for a while / second / a minute.
Sit in order.
No running / shouting.
No pushing.
No talking.
Time's up.
Faster.
Sit on your bottom.
Sit still.
Don't move the chair.
Don't squeak / drag the chair.
Please have / get your books ready before I come in.
Textbook out, please. / Get your books out.
Please put away your comic books.
How come you forgot to bring your book?
Don't forget to bring your book next time.
Those who haven't got their books, share it with your partners.
Everyone, attention now. / Please listen! / Your attention, please. / Can I have your attention?

Concentrate! This is important.
Eyes on the speaker. / Look at me. / Look at the speaker.
Look this way.
Look here. / Look over here.
Look to the left. / Look to your right.
Face the rear.
Nobody moves.
Don't move. / Freeze. / Stay where you are.
Sit straight and don't move.
Hands on heads.
Shh! Don't whisper.
Quiet, please! / Please be quiet. / Keep silent, please.
Stop talking. / Don't talk. / Don't say a word now.
You'd better stop chatting.
Please shut your mouth.
I'm not finished yet.
Let me finish talking, please.
What's important?
Over there; what's so funny?
Somebody is still chatting.
We need to move in a line.
Please line up. / Please get in a line. / Get into a queue.
Stand in two lines. / Make two lines.

I want four lines. Please line up in numerical order.
Go to the very end of the line.
Dinner will be served when you finish lining up.
I'll see which group is the best at standing in line.
Don't cut in line. / Don't cut in. / Don't jump in line.
Now, move quickly and try not to make any noise as you move.
Don't run. Walk slowly.
Nobody speaks in the corridor.
Be careful when you go up and down the stairs.
Everybody, go to the lab now!
Is the sound clear at the back?
Can you hear the sound clearly?
The volume is too low. We can't hear you at the back.
Is it loud enough now?
Please turn up / down the volume.
We're going to watch a video clip.
Please draw the curtains.
Don't touch the lens.
Don't look into the lamp because it's too bright.
It's out of order.
I think it's broken.
That's strange. There's no sound.
We've got a bad connection.

| Lights out, please. / Turn on / off all the lights, please. |
| Stop that sound. / Please stop making that sound. |
| Please don't tap the desk. |
| Please don't stamp your feet on the floor. |
| Your desk is messy. |
| Please tidy your desks. / Clean up your desks. |
| Let's tidy up before we start the lesson. |
| Put your things away. |
| Straighten up your desks. |
| Please clean the blackboard. |
| Please empty the bin. |

7. 课堂教学 Classroom Teaching – Teaching

| Which page are we on? / Where are we at? |
| We're slightly behind schedule. Let's speed up. |
| We're on page 32. |
| Let's start from the third paragraph on page 32. |
| Good, we're just on schedule. We're right on track. |
| We have a very tight schedule. |
| We're falling behind. |
| We'll need some makeup classes. |
| We have no time to lose. |

We have to hurry.
Do you remember what we learned last time / in our previous lesson?
You're right. Anything else?
Can anybody tell me what they were?
Let's go over / run through it again.
Before we start, let's have a short / brief review of our previous lesson.
What do you remember the most from our previous lesson?
Let's see how much you can remember from the last lesson?
Put your hand up if you remember.
You really did a good job last time.
Do you have any questions about what we learned last time?
What's the title of today's lesson?
Can you guess what we're going to learn today through the title?
Who knows what the title means?
Here's what we're going to do today. / Here are the things we'll be learning today.
We'll finish off Lesson 10 today.
We'll play a game today.
We'll be doing some reading and writing.
These are the goals for today's lesson.
The goals for today's lesson are as follows.
First, we will be able to make questions.
Second, we will be able to write an email.

Everybody, please keep these goals in mind.

Let's make sure that we achieve all the goals.

Now that we know our goals, let's get started.

It would be better if we sing a song before we start.

Let's do some stretching before starting off.

Let's yawn with a stretch.

What do you know about this topic?

Let's watch an exciting video before we take a look at the story.

Let's make a world map.

Let's start with an interesting story.

It's time to get to the point.

It's reading time. Am I right?

Are you ready to move on to the activity?

We're on Lesson 10 today, right?

Please go to page 65. / Flip over to page 65.

Take out your books and open them at page 65.

On which page does Lesson 10 start? It's on page 65.

Let's move on to the next page.

Let's go back to where we were.

It's at the top / bottom. / It's in the middle.

It's on the left. / It's on the right-hand side.

It's in the upper / lower left / right corner.

It's to the left of the picture.

It's two lines from the top.
Find line 6.
We are on line 6 on page 22.
It's the sixth line from the bottom. / It's six lines up from the bottom.
Go up six lines.
Take a handout as you go out.
Please have your parents sign this handout and bring it back.
Did anyone get two by mistake?
I didn't prepare enough for everyone. / I haven't prepared enough for everyone.
Do you have a copy?
Who hasn't got one?
There should be one for every two people.
I have much to write on the blackboard / whiteboard today.
I won't rub it off, so please copy it during the break.
We've run out of chalk / markers.
You have nice handwriting.
Please clean the board.
Rub off everything, please.
Don't erase it yet.
Could you get me the board eraser?
It's time for a quiz. / Let's take a quiz.
Though it's a test, there's no need to worry.

I won't grade the scores.
The scores will be graded.
It's one point for each question.
Please clear your desks.
Get a piece of paper ready.
Please take a sheet and pass the rest to the back.
Have you all got the test paper?
You have to fill in the blanks with the right answer.
Don't cheat, and sit up straight.
I'll call out the answers.
Exchange your test papers with your partners and mark them.
Let's wrap up. / It's time to wrap up. / Let's sum up what we have learnt.
Shall we wrap up? / Shall we reflect upon today's lesson?
Who can summarize today's lesson?
Is there anything that you don't understand from today's lesson?
Let's review today's lesson.
Did we accomplish our goals?

8. 作业检查 Homework Check

Time to check homework.
Please take out / show me your homework.
Flip the pages so that I can check your homework.
I'll stamp your homework.

Please show me the very last page of your homework.
Please pass your homework to the front.
The ones who sitting at the back, please gather all the homework.
The last person in the row, please collect the homework.
Submit your homework to the class president.
I'm not receiving any homework from this moment on.
Was the deadline too soon?
Stay behind after school and do your homework.
As for homework, memorize this dialogue.
Practise your roles at home.
Until next time, be sure to practise the expressions.
I'm going to check your homework in our next lesson.
We need some supplies next time.
Please bring some leaves for the next class.
We're going to make cards, so what do we need?
Please have scissors, glue and some colored paper ready.
Pack your supplies as soon as you get home.
Let's call it a day. / That's all for today.
I think we've done enough today.
I hope you found this lesson useful and interesting.
Enjoy your lunch / holiday / weekend.
Until next time, take care.

9. 英语技能 English Skills

Let me show you how to play the game.
Let me demonstrate it first.
Watch me carefully. / Watch me first. / Watch me doing it. / I'll show you first.
Copy me. / Follow what I'm doing.
Nice try.
Wait! It's not your turn yet.
One at a time.
Who hasn't had a go yet?
I'll be with you in a minute.
You'll only have ten minutes for this activity.
Please stick to the time limit.
Don't rush.
Take your time.
How many minutes do we have left?
There's two minutes left. Wrap up. / Finish off, please.
Hurry up. / Speed up.
Hurry, we have no time to lose.
We don't have much / enough time.
Let's move on.
Let's go to next activity.
It's break time. / Time for a break. / Let's take / have a break.
It's OK to make errors / mistakes.

It's OK if the grammar is wrong.
You don't have to worry if your pronunciation is not good.
Answer in a complete sentence, please.
For example, you should answer "It's a dog," instead of "dog".
Say it all together. / Everybody, all together.
Watch your pronunciation when you speak.
Say it like this.
Am I speaking too fast?
What do you say in this case?
How do you say 图画 in English?
Is there any other way of saying it?
Keep practising until you memorize it.
Practise in pairs.
First, front rows only. Are you ready?
Change all the verbs into the past tense.
Any topic will do.
Read what it says.
Which page are we reading? I'm on page 12.
Please write neatly so that others can read your writing easily. My handwriting is really awful.
Try not to scribble.
Please fill in the blank. What's the word that goes in the blank?
Explain your idea.

How do you read this word? / How do you pronounce it?
This word is misspelled.
You missed a letter.
You should add / take out an "r" here.
What's the preposition that goes with the verb "depend"? By? No, think harder. I have no idea. It's "on", like in "It depends on you."
Which article do you think will go in here?
Which pronoun can go in this blank?

小结、反思与练习
Summary, Reflection and Practice

教师教学用语的重要性不言而喻。教学用语不仅直接作用于教师教学效果，也可以让学生通过模仿习得这些标准地道的英语。

☐ The importance of teacher talk is self-evident.

☐ The refined language that a teacher uses, definitely and effectively enhances the teaching quality, besides being a model for students to imitate in the classroom.

For example, the word "can" is often used incorrectly instead of the word "may" when people ask "Can I go to the toilet?" The word "may" is requesting permission while "can" is asking if a person has the ability to do a task. Of course, they have the ability to go to the toilet, but they are asking for permission so they should say, "May I go to the toilet, please?"

For another example, the words "get" and "take" are often confused by non-native speakers. "Get" is used to bring something to where the speaker is, while "take" is used to carry something away from the speaker.

The listed common expressions above are for your reference.

小结 Your summary

1.

2.

3.

反思 Reflection

1. I continue to be challenged by ...

2. My spoken English ...

3. My instruction in the classroom ...

练习 Practice

1.

2.

3.

教研团队练习 Group Discussion：

1.分组讨论教学准备（Discuss）

2.分组进行案例分享（Share）

3.分组开展讨论应用（Apply）

课后篇

After Teaching

第五章

实时反馈的评估与反思

In & After Class – Assessment and Reflection

评估，可分为终结性评估（summative assessment）和过程性评估（formative assessment）。终结性评估是在一个教学阶段或周期结束时进行的总结性或终极性评估，就是众人常见的一次考试定结果，不重视或很少关心其过程；而过程性评估又名形成性评估，是在教学过程中进行的过程性或发展性评估，比如单元小测验、教学项目汇报等，可根据教学目标、教学内容采用不同的评估手段跟踪教学过程、检查并巩固教学效果、实时反馈教学信息。很多（国外）大学在招生时，会综合考虑该生进入大学前几年在高中的各种表现，其实就是在综合使用过程性评估与终结性评估。近年来，形成性评估越来越受到重视，也被广泛地运用到更多的教学场景中。本章节主要阐述教师个体在教学中常常使用的教学评估与反思的方式和方法。

At the end of a lesson, an effective teacher will give students time to reflect upon the lesson. An effective teacher sets high expectations even upon themselves.

She wants every child to achieve success, but she also needs to be kind and understanding of herself. Perhaps the lesson was at the end of the day and the children were tired. Maybe, she, herself, wasn't feeling well or was exhausted.

Did they achieve the success criteria? Have they had an opportunity to show what they have learnt? Do they think that they have achieved the stated objectives? This time allows students to pause in their thinking and construct where they are now in their journey. They could then be involved in determining the next steps in their learning. This feedback will help them to progress.

了解学生学习的掌握情况只是其一，教师如何根据评估反馈相应调整教学同样重要。搜集信息只是通往目的地的手段或途径而已。It is what we then do as a result of this gleaned knowledge that drives assessment and makes it a learning tool. An effective teacher uses this information to feed into their lesson planning. Constantly assessing through various means empowers the teacher to engage effectively with where students are at and enables them to be led to the next step. This is teaching at its best.

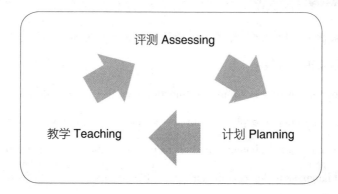

如前图所示，只有在教学中通过各种方式和方法不断地评估测评，然后相应地制定出恰当的教学计划，最后在教学实践中实施，才能不断提升教学效果。如此循环往复，成就最佳教学。

1. 终结性评估 Summative Assessment

书面考试常常被认为是评测学生学习效果的唯一方式，其实不然。不管是quizzes，tests，还是exams，考试的目的就是评估，了解学生的已知或未知情况（*a diagnosis of what students knew or didn't know at a certain point in time.*）。这可能就是很多老师把评估等同于书面考试的原因。其实，考试只是评估学生学习效果的一种方式，这里我们重点探讨如何结合过程性评估来提高教学效果。

2. 过程性评估 Formative Assessment

过程性评估的方式灵活多样。

① 课堂记录 Record

记录学生在口语表达中常见的语法错误，进行分析，然后有的放矢地对这些错误进行再教学。

Students' responses to an oral question can also be recorded to guide re-teaching. For example, explain to me how I can get to a nearby shopping centre from the school gate. In listening to their responses on the recording, I can analyse their oral language to detect common grammatical errors.

This error analysis can also be used after giving students a written task. By carefully looking at the mistakes that have been made, common errors become obvious and this Knowledge should immediately feed forward to the next lesson or lessons.

② 集体评阅 Peer Assessment

如果班级不大，可以让学生在班级分享他们的写作。写作任务要简洁明了，写几个句子就好。学生与老师围坐在一起，把作业放在中间，然后一起来对作业进行集体评阅。可采用以下步骤：

Step 1: Look at the first student's work together, noting whether they have used a capital letter at the beginning of each sentence and a full stop at the end.

Step 2: Place a tick ✓ (check mark) for each of these things.

Step 3: Discuss if there is a verb in each sentence. In English, every sentence has a verb. Give a tick ✓ for each verb.

Step 4: Also discuss if the sentence makes sense.

如果班级规模较大，每次先就几位同学的写作进行上述步骤，这样学生就知道正确的句子应该是什么样的。这个方法同样也向学生展示了如何修改编辑他们的作文。通过分析写作样本，高效能教师能精确评测出学生常犯的错误，并在随后的课堂教学中加以解决。

③ 游戏评估 Games

Games can be used as an effective assessment tool as well. By keeping a written or mental checklist as you observe students in a game situation, you can easily assess who is having difficulties or which students have no problems in a set task.

Here are a few examples.

游戏一：

Ask students to write a sound or a combination sound, such as "th" or "sh", or even a word. You could divide the class into teams with one child from each team given a different coloured whiteboard mark. These children write their answers on a large whiteboard in the front of the class, before returning to their teams; or the teams each have their own small whiteboard on which to write and this is held up and taken to the teacher with the required answer.

游戏二：

Another team game would be to jumble letters and ask students to organize them into a given word. This idea can also be extended to sentences. Sentences are cut up into words and given to students in groups for them to unjumble. The sentence may or may not be told to them beforehand. It could be a clue, given a short time later if they are having difficulty. This can quickly diagnose students who are having difficulty with English word order.

游戏三：

I have also played many oral discrimination games to test how students are hearing sounds. For example, the TPR activity to discriminate between short and long vowels (Page 111). The children have to run to the side which corresponds to the sound used. By watching how swiftly they respond, I can quickly assess which students know the difference between the short vowel and the long vowel.

游戏四：

I have also put flashcards with the different vowels on the floor or on the walls around the teaching area. When I say a word, they have to run to the corresponding vowel. Again, this is a tool to ascertain their knowledge.

以上提及的几种简单实用的游戏评估方法，可以随机根据需要针对不同层次的学生在课堂教学中使用。对于有一定英语基础的学生，我经常用的是jumble sentences这个游戏（*Sentences are cut up into words and given to students in groups for them to unjumble*）。教师可以根据学生玩的情况（快慢、正误等）来增加或降低这个游戏的难度，甚至是趣味性。针对更小的学生，可以用拼组某一群体词（如人体部位），甚至只是拼组某一个单词。

④ 检查单 Checklists

检查单非常实用，几乎在各行各业都可以看到。Checklists are commonly used in lines of work. By reminding us of what to teach or how to teach, checklists are especially applied to teaching and learning assessments.

检查单1用于上课之前。教师可以根据自己需要或经验体会自行添加删减，逐渐形成自己的风格。以attention grabber为例，高效能教师都有自己独特的口令或方法，让学生迅速集中注意力。

Checklist 1 : Before Teaching Checklist

Put a tick ✓ in the box beside each section when it is ready.

		Ready to Teach
	1	Ready to teach mentally
	2	Planning (aims, objectives, materials, methodologies, assessment, etc.)
	3	Teaching equipment and facilities
	4	Students' background information (names, sex, competency, temperament, etc.)
	5	Environment establishment (function area, decoration)
	6	Rules and agreements (Rule posters can be seen easily and clearly. Students can read them at any time.)
	7	Attention Grabber (Determine one attention grabber.)

检查单还可以用于某些教学环节，比如下列检查单2、3、4、5，分别就某一单项教学内容（颜色、数字、教室内物品、单字母发音）（*Colours, numbers, various labels of objects around the classroom and knowledge of the single letter sounds*）的掌握进行了评估。A simple tick (✓) or checkmark is placed in the appropriate column to show if a student displays that knowledge. 教师同样可以根据自己需要进行检查单的设计。

Checklist 2 : Assessment of Learning Colors

Colour \ Names	Daniel Li	Lucy Kim	Victor Wei
Red			
Yellow			
Blue			
Green			
Purple			
Orange			
Black			
White			
Pink			
Brown			

Checklist 3 : Assessment of Learning Numbers

Number \ Names	Daniel Li	Lucy Kim	Victor Wei
1-9			
10-20			
In 5s			
In 10s			
In 100s			
37-51			
In 2s			
backwards			

Checklist 4 : Assessment of Learning Objects

Objects / Names	Daniel Li	Lucy Kim	Victor Wei
desk			
chair			
computer			
floor			
pencil			
book			
whiteboard			
pen			
crayon			

Checklist 5 : Assessment of Learning Sounds

Student Name	Single Letter sounds (Score out of 26)	Weaknesses
Student A	21	vowels + y, w.
Student B	25	a / e
Student C	26	
Student D	26	
Student E	24	a / e / i
Student F	17	vowels + r, l, x, w, q
Student G	18	vowels + m / n, x, v, q
Student H	16	vowels + r / l, g, y, w, q

The above figure, Checklist 5, shows the recorded data flowing from a particular quiz, in which students' knowledge of the single letter sounds was tested. By recording the information on this checklist, I was able to quickly see how well students knew the single letter sounds and what the common errors were for further instruction. I could divide the class into groups with those who knew the sounds well working on another task of blending sounds into words while I taught focused lessons on "x", "v", "y" to selected students. This differentiated learning is an effective consequence of using data.

如检查单5所示，教师根据学生掌握的情况可以进行分层教学。

作为教师，记录追踪学生的进步成长非常重要。A spreadsheet or mark book provides proof as to whether the children are improving in their knowledge as a result of your teaching. It can also help to determine what teaching should then follow. Perhaps some students will need to be retaught some things while other students can move ahead with their learning.

检查单6，为学年开始的8月8日，对三位同学就他们的听音写字母能力进行的评测。In Checklist 6 showing Phonics Assessment, Child C only made two errors, while the other two children (A and B) made 5 errors in the 8th August initial assessment. During the pursuing weeks, I taught the unknown sounds and continued to teach digraphs or combination sounds, such as "sh", "ch", "ay" and "oi".

Checklist 6 : Phonics Assessment

Assessment Time	Out of total	Student A	Student B	Student C
8 Aug Single Letter Sounds	25	20	20	23
1 Oct Single letter sounds	25	25	25	25
3rd Oct Digraphs	14	14	13	13
3 Oct CVC words	6	3	3	2
29 Nov Digraphs	24	24	23	23
29 Nov Spell rules	6	5	1	3
7 Mar Digraphs	30	30	29	30
8 April Single sounds + Digraphs	25 + 5	20 + 1	25 + 3	24 + 0

八周后，再次对他们的听音写字母能力进行了评测。All three students demonstrated that they had mastered this knowledge in the subsequent assessment on 1st October. They also knew how to write most of the digraphs which had been taught.

11月29日，快到学期末时，又对他们进行了评测。By the 29th November, the children could write 23 of the 24 digraphs that had been taught. However, the test results also revealed that one child could not apply the taught spelling rules of silent "e". Consequently, this governed what I should do next. Another 10 weeks later, the children had mastered all of the digraphs that I had taught; so, my focus shifted from phonics to sentence development.

When marking any phonics test, I always use tally marks on my master copy to track which sounds need to be revisited. This information guides my next lessons.

检查单7，可以用来让学生进行自我评测。这个检查单共列出了6大维度16个检测点，不仅仅是给学生自我评测，也是在提醒学生学习上需要掌握的维度。Checklists are also a useful tool for students to ensure they achieve their goals. A simple checklist can provide a way to check if they have completed set tasks by breaking them down into manageable bites. In this way, checklists can scaffold students' learning as in the example below from "6+1 Traits of Writing" by Ruth Culham (2016)[①].

---

① Ruth Culham. *6+1 Traits of Writing: The Complete Guide for the Primary Grades; Theory and Practice*. New York: Scholastic US. 2016.

Checklist 7 : Student Self-Assessment A

6 Traits Checklist: K2 – Grade 2

Ideas:

- ☐ My writing tells the story.
- ☐ I stay on topic.
- ☐ I have included details in my writing.

Organization:

- ☐ My work has a title.
- ☐ I have a beginning, a middle and end.
- ☐ I have thought about who, what, when, where and why.
- ☐ My sentences flow.

Voice:

- ☐ My writing sounds like me.
- ☐ My reader will know what I think.
- ☐ I have included details in my writing.

Word Choice:

- ☐ I use interesting words to tell my story.
- ☐ My words give the reader a picture in their head.

Sentence fluency:

- ☐ I have reread my work to check if it makes sense or not.

Conventions:

- ☐ I have spelled my sight words correctly.
- ☐ I have sounded out words I don't know.
- ☐ I have used capitals and full stops.

If students actively take part in planning a rubric or checklist by determining what will be the success criteria for a set assignment, they are more likely to feel part of the process and take ownership of its impact upon themselves.

有时可以邀请学生来共同制作检查评测单。比如，让学生在全班面前背诵诗歌时。In Checklist 8 below, not only did the students determine the criteria for the checklist, but they were asked to assess their peers using it. Each student was given the Evaluation of Oral Poetry Presentation worksheet below (See Checklist 8), on which to record their assessments. We then discussed each student's performance against the rubric as a whole class, thus enabling each student to take away how they could improve.

这让学生有主人翁的角色感，他们会积极地利用检查单来进行自主学习。This criteria-based assessment allows students to develop ownership for their learning as they actively use the checklist tool.

Checklist 8：Student Self-Assessment B

Your name: _____

Evaluation of Oral Poetry Presentation

Scoring

2 = did it all the time

1 = did it sometimes

0 = did NOT do it at all

Reciter's Name: _____

Criteria	Score
Looks at the audience.	
Says the words loudly.	
Uses expression in their voice.	
Speaks without hesitation. (Knows all the sentences.)	

⑤ 报告单Report

报告单常用于汇报。每次评测之后，应该把学生的学习情况及时向家长报告。A report is also commonly used after assessment, in order to report to parents the outcome or results based on children's performance at a particular point in time.

报告单1是汇报二年级学生A当前学习表现优异的地方，以及当前在读和写方面正在努力的目标。

Report 1：Student A's Strengths & Goals

Student Sample A　Grade 2

ESL Strengths & Goals

3 Way Conferences 1st November

Strengths:

- Listen attentively
- Fluent speaker
- Reads expressively

Current Goals:

Reading:

To ask thinking questions to himself about the story as he reads.

To read accurately including articles, and suffixes (-ed, -s, etc).

Writing:

To continue to develop his spelling accuracy.

To write using consistent tenses.

To ensure singular or plural subjects agree with the verb.

To re-read his writing to ensure it makes sense.

Comments: _____

_____

_____

　　报告单2，是汇报一年级学生B当前学习表现优异的地方，以及当前在读、写、说方面正在努力的目标。

Report 2 : Student B's Strengths & Goals

Student Sample B Grade 1

ESL Strengths & Goals

3 Way Conferences 23rd February

Strengths:

- Listens quietly
- Observant

Current Goals:

Reading:

To pronounce accurately words with the letter r .

To retell stories with all the details by herself.

Writing:

To write more punctuated sentences independently.

To leave spaces after every word.

Speaking:

To contribute to class discussions more frequently.

To answer questions without being asked directly.

Comments: _____

_____

_____

报告单3，是汇报学生A在听、说、读、写、看等方面的表现，以及仍需要提高的方面。

Report 3 : Sample of Typical Comments for Report Writing

Student A is able to:

Listening

- Listen attentively.
- Follow one-step instructions.
- Follow multi-step instructions.
- Follow simple instructions, commands and directions.
- Understand oral messages.
- Help friends to understand class instructions.

Speaking

- Respond to routine questions using new words that have been learnt.
- Count from 1 to 10 in English.
- Sing English songs with the teacher.
- Remember new words.
- Answer questions using new words.
- Answer questions using single words.
- Answer questions using simple phrases or short sentences.
- Speak with a clear voice.
- Repeat words.
- Repeat words and sentences.
- Retell stories with the teacher's support.
- Retell stories with the support of pictures.
- Retell a story using her own words and sentences.
- Express herself clearly in front of the class.
- Use a given sentence pattern to express ideas.

Reading

- Read simple English picture books independently.

- Read English story books with the teacher's support.

- Read given materials independently.

- Answer recall questions about the text.

- Understand the main ideas in English storybooks.

- Recognize basic English vocabulary.

- Recognize the English words for numbers 1-10.

- Identify English words for colours and parts of the body.

- Read and understand simple stories with visual clues.

- Read picture books related to the topic.

- Label pictures with given vocabulary.

- Recognize keywords related to the topic.

Writing

- Copy words and sentences using given examples.

- Complete simple sentences from a bank of words.

- Write the day and date in English.

- Write simple sentences independently.

- Write correct simple sentences using given examples.

- Work independently.

- Focus on a set task.

- Complete written work on time.

Viewing

- Understand and respond to illustrations, visual messages and ICT (Information Communication Technology) iconography in different media.

- Access information by following visual clues.

- Create simple, visual presentations.

- Reflect appropriately on presentations.

- Understand information from a given picture.

- Sequence pictures about stories.

The student needs to:

- Watch and listen English stories and songs online at home.

- Interact with native English speakers during play time.

- Participate actively in class discussions.

- Practise the words that have been learnt using Quizlet.

- Work more slowly and carefully.

- Follow class instructions.

- Work more independently.

- Focus and complete tasks on time.

- Listen to instructions more carefully.

- Speak slowly and clearly.

- Communicate personal needs in English.

- Answer more questions in class.

- Speak in sentences.

- Speak more loudly.

- Improve his retelling of stories.

- Read more English picture books at home.

- Practise handwriting.

- Write complete sentences.

报告单4，是根据学习目标来汇报学生（Mary）在听、说、读、写等方面的表现和评价。

Report 4：A Sample Comment Report Based on Objectives

Objectives

Children show their understanding by:

Listening

- following simple instructions, commands and directions.
- listening with sustained concentration in different contexts.

Speaking

- articulating words clearly.
- asking and responding to simple questions, expressing her own ideas.

Reading

- reading and understanding words, phrases and simple sentences with visual clues.
- demonstrating understanding of the meaning of words and the text.

Writing

- writing sentences on various topics using mostly correct spelling and punctuation and appropriate tenses.
- using a variety of descriptive vocabulary to enhance their writing.

报告样本

A Sample Comment Report based on the above objectives

(Mary) happily participates in all the activities in the ESL classroom, immediately following simple instructions. She listens to stories with sustained concentration and clearly articulates poems and songs that she has learnt in class.

(Mary) asks and responds to simple questions, expressing her own ideas and opinions in discussions. Although her oral sentences have grammatical errors, she willingly tries her best.

(Mary) is reading simple stories with visual clues and demonstrates a good understanding of the story. I would encourage her to keep reading every day for her own pleasure as this will develop her fluency and vocabulary.

(Mary) uses her growing knowledge of phonics to spell many one or two syllable words. Her memory of high frequency words is developing well. Consequently, (Mary) is beginning to write sentences on various topics with correct spelling and punctuation. She now needs to focus on adding more descriptive vocabulary with the appropriate verb tenses.

---

⑥ 档案袋 Portfolio

档案袋的作用超出了我们最初的设想。过去，对艺术类学生的最后评测就是让其展示自己的作品。通过呈现一系列作品，他们甚至可以直接被大学录取或者被公司聘用。

近些年来，西方教育一直在鼓励教师帮助学生就自己过去一年的学习情况建立档案袋。The student places selected pieces of writing, work samples, test worksheets and photographs of various things they have done into an organized folder. In this way, any child can show their progress in learning.

档案袋的形式可以是多样化的。These portfolios could take the form of a display book and an on-line website, in which PowerPoints, slides and student-created media could be presented.

If it is to be useful, a clear purpose for the portfolio is paramount. Each piece of work should be selected to show what a child can do at a particular point in time. It is a tool to demonstrate his / her learning and progress over a set time period.

鼓励学生自主为自己的档案袋挑选喜欢的作品。If a student is encouraged to take ownership for the selection and presentation of his portfolio, it can become a useful assessment tool as the student reflects upon his work. Then, with the assistance and guidance of an effective teacher, it can aid students to determine the next goal for their further development.

The primary audience for these educational portfolios consists of the student, the teacher and their parents. This is why the sharing of the portfolio is often an integral part of student-teacher-parent conferences in the western educational world.

学生独立自选，不仅帮助教师减轻了筛选需要花费大量时间和精力的压力，也激励了学生自主独立意识。While portfolios can be time-consuming to organize and maintain for a busy teacher, if the student is actively involved, they can be a powerful evaluation tool both to the student and to their teacher.

以下Portfolio 1和Portfolio 2是学生的电子档案。教师可以制作或帮助学生制作关于某个教学活动或某个教学阶段的档案袋。随着档案袋的丰盈，那种满满的成就感，不仅令学生内心满足，教师和家长也倍感欣慰。

Portfolio 1：Student A's E-Portfolio

The student had to write a reflection on how he was displaying different attitudes. At this stage of the student's English language development, he was asked to complete given sentences. Here is his unedited response.

PYP Attitudes	
Attitude	**Reflection**
Well balanced	I am well balanced because I eat healthy lunch everyday.
Principled	I am principled, when I did wrong things in school I said the truth.
Inquirer	I know

The below reflection was completed by a young English language learner in a Performing Arts class, following his performance with his class in a school concert. Again, he was asked to complete given sentence starters.

Semester One Reflection
(T) The thing I liked most about our concert:
(S) The thing I liked most about playing a triangle was everyone looked at me.
(T) The thing I think I could improve:
(S) I will sing better so that others can hear me.

Portfolio 2 : Student B's E-Portfolio

The below figure, Sharing The Planet, shows an assessment piece typed on a computer to show a student's understanding of concepts, after the class had completed an inquiry into how animals and their habitats are connected. This was written independently by a young student after a year of English language study.

Sharing the Planet

Central idea: Animals and their habitats are connected.

Line of inquiry: Needs of animals.

Animals need sun and water to survive.

They need trees and grass for making houses and they eat leaves and grass.

Clouds give rain for plant to grow and water for animals to drink.

说起档案袋，必须得再次提及一下曾被人称为"全世界最好的学前班"的瑞吉欧·艾米里亚教育体系[1]。瑞吉欧教育体系对记录文件（documentation）特别重视。瑞吉欧跟随孩子发展需求，为孩子设置或研制个性化教育方案。他们总是选择孩子喜欢的主题，以孩子为主体，让孩子用"一百种语言"来表达自己。对于孩子的学习活动探索都有记录（documentation），而记录本身已经远远不是对孩子学习结果的一种单纯评价依据，更是一种有效的教学方式和方法。

3. 反思 Reflection

Story 14：A TPR Story

I attended a seminar about different teaching methodologies a few years ago. Among those presented, TPR was very impressive.

I couldn't wait to go back to school and put it into practice; and it was so successful that my class transformed into chaos. I did design my class with reference to what I learned at the seminar. It was almost perfect with the required nouns, verbs, and basic sentences. I introduced what we would learn to the students in a clear and concise manner. Every student looked very excited. The nouns for that day included "horse", while the verbs included "ride". After learning the sentence patterns, the

---

[1] 每个孩子都有一百种语言，来自于瑞吉欧创立人马拉古奇的一首诗。Loris Malaguzzi, founder of the Reggio Approach, describes the "infinite ways that children can express, explore, and connect their thoughts, feelings and imaginings."

children were asked to apply what they learned immediately using TPR. They could play freely in groups. As a result, all the children in groups were "riding the horse", and they kept telling me "I ride the horse" while riding around the classroom. Everyone burst into laughter and played excitedly. My classroom looked like a racecourse, and to me it was out of control.

I was very frustrated. Then I reflected what the problem was. I thought that nothing was wrong with TPR; the only problem might be that the children were too excited and active in class. So, would it be much better to use another pedagogy instead of TPR in their next class?

As usual I did a review of the previous lesson the next day. To my surprise, the children remembered the vocabulary they learned that day even though it had been chaos. They remembered 100%, which I could never have imagined. Usually they could hardly remember half of the vocabulary I listed and taught.

The result forced me to reflect again. Was my last class a total failure? It seemed not, even though it had appeared to be in chaos. Yes, it was a bit out of my control, but the result proved it was effective; so effective that the result was far beyond my expectations.

So, I analyzed my last class again, thinking what I could do to improve the order and organization instead of mess and chaos. My time management could be improved when assigning the TPR activity, and the rules should be emphasized before the task began.

I redesigned another TPR in other grades. It turned out to be another success, but without chaos.

古人云：吾日三省吾身。上述教学案例也是教师对失控的课堂进行反思的故事。课后反思对教师改进教学方法十分必要。After the students have left, a wise teacher will reflect upon the lesson. What went well? Were the objectives really achieved by all of the students? Why did something not work? Was it because I was trying to fit too much into the lesson? Was a particular activity not appropriate for the level of the students' abilities? How could the lesson have been improved?

Perhaps the most important questions to pose at the end of the lesson are: What should be the next steps? Does part of the lesson need to be repeated in a different way for some students? How can this be done so that the students, who achieved the objectives, will continue to be challenged? An effective teacher is always learning from what takes place and using it to feed forward into the next steps for her students. Thus, planning and teaching make up a continual, cyclical process.

小结、反思与练习
Summary, Reflection and Practice

高效能教师常常会给自己设定更高目标，进而也就有了更高要求。反思之余，也要善待和理解自己教学上的得与失。Since she wants every student to achieve their potential, she will also reflect upon her own teaching, setting high expectations upon herself. Oftentimes, a conscientious teacher will blame herself for a poor lesson, but she also needs to be kind towards and understanding of herself. Perhaps the lesson was at the end of the day and the children were tired. Maybe, she, herself, wasn't feeling well or was exhausted.

总之，教学评估并非是单一的考试（期末笔试或口试），还包括多种多样的过程性评估。高效能教师要学会灵活地运用上述评估方式。

终结性评估：考试、测评

过程性评估：

☐ 课堂记录 Record

☐ 集体评阅 Peer assessment

☐ 游戏评估 Games

· 小组游戏 Team games

· 白板游戏 Small whiteboards games

- 组字成词 Jumble letters into words / 组词成句 Jumble words into sentences / 组句成段 Jumble sentences into paragraph / 组句成段 sentences into paragraph
- 元音区分 Vowel discrimination

☐ 检查单 Checklist

☐ 报告单 Report

☐ 档案袋 Portfolio

Both assessment and reflection promote teaching and learning. It is necessary to make up or even reteach knowledge or skills after finding out the weaknesses through assessment. Teachers should thrive upon reflection.

小结 Your summary

1. _____

_____

2. _____

_____

3. _____

_____

反思 Reflection

1. My class ...

2. The principal ...

3. I really love ...

练习 Practice

1. _____

_____

2. _____

_____

3. _____

_____

教研团队练习 Group Discussion：

1.分组讨论教学准备（Discuss）

_____

_____

2.分组进行案例分享（Share）

_____

_____

3.分组开展讨论应用（Apply）

_____

_____

顺畅、高效的沟通与交流
Communicating

　　沟通与交流非常重要，但是很多人并没有完全意识到这一点。无论是日常人际关系还是职场协作，很多时候，问题或麻烦都是因为不会说话或交流不畅引起的。作为教师，沟通与交流是一门必修课。古人云祸从口出，就是告诫我们说话要特别谨慎。又曰沉默是金，告诉我们少说话，言多必失。但是，作为教师，日常沟通交流又必不可少，沉默是金是告诫我们尽量少说话别乱说话，不是不说话，而是要会说话。沟通能力是可以学习和训练培养的。下面用一些实际案例来看看，如何与学生、家长进行正确的沟通和交流。

　　每个学生都是父母家人的宝贝。教师每天与他们打交道，稍不小心传递了一点关于孩子的令人不悦的迹象，这些父母便会非常敏感，内心不安。所以，我们必须从一开始就要与每个家庭和家长建立正面、积极的合作关系。

　　A very old English expression describes someone who is cherished above all others to be "the apple of their eye". In other words, each child is the apple of their parents' eyes, because they bring parents such great joy, purpose and happiness.

Teachers are daily interacting with these treasured lives and when we communicate anything even slightly negative about them to their parents, we can expect the parents to be very sensitive. Therefore, we must be careful to build up a positive relationship with the families right from the beginning of the school year.

首先，我们要诚实地让父母知道学生的实际情况。Remember, that you are dealing with the apple of their eye; so, you need to be gentle but also honest. Speak the truth with a heart of love for the child. Don't be in a hurry. This will take time.

未雨绸缪，不要让问题升级。Don't allow a problem to escalate before action is taken. Nip it in the bud. If a child is causing disruptions in the class because of social or emotional problems, the parents will need to be informed. A face to face meeting is often the best course of action so that you can answer any immediate questions and explain the situation fully.

若学生在某些学习方面有困难，让家长了解到你已采取的措施和已取得的成效。Prepare your evidence well. If a child is having difficulties with reading comprehension, have a recent test which shows this. If they are finding it hard to express their own ideas in writing, show them what you have tried to do to help them.

若要面谈或联系家长，请清晰地告诉家长他们要如何协助学生，以便在做好家校沟通的基础上，达成家校合作联盟。Have a clear purpose in bringing parents in for an interview or contacting them. Prepare clear steps that they can do to assist. This will help to increase their confidence in your professionalism.

When children are not progressing as they should, it can be very difficult to determine whether the issue is a language learning difficulty or a more systemic learning problem. One of the best ways to help in your diagnosis, is to see how well they are learning in their home or first language.

Ask the child to write a story using their home language. Then engage the help of another speaker of that same language, preferably a teacher, who can determine if the writing is up to the developmental level of other children of the same age in that home language. A short reading comprehension task could be set in the home language to get further information. If the difficulty is simply related to learning a new language, his work in his home language should be comparable to his home language peers. However, if his home language work is weak, the evidence points to deeper underlying learning issues.

1. 书面交流 Written Communication

书面交流是家校沟通的重要方式，比如写一封信或电邮，见Written Communication 1 : 一封欢迎信。Letting the parents know that you are professional and taking your job seriously will help them have confidence in you. I would often take the time to email or write an introductory welcome letter to them during the first week of the school year.

Written Communication 1: An Introductory Welcome Letter

Dear parents of Diane,

It has been my pleasure to meet Diane, who has joined our Withdrawal Level ESL class. I am Mrs Vaughan and I will continue to work with your child this semester.

You have already seen the ESL Special Reading Booklet that I have made for her. This will be sent home after each lesson and needs to be returned each day, as I will be putting different poems, songs or stories in it from time to time. Please enjoy these with your child.

It will be wonderful if you can take the time to listen to your child read every day. This is the biggest help with learning a new language.

The Lexia program is also a big help. Please encourage your child to use this for fifteen minutes three times a week. Details have been sent home with your child in a separate letter.

I have also made a website on which I have placed some videos and information to support your child. Please let me know if you have trouble accessing it. The Phonics with Mrs. Vaughan videos are also on YouTube. Please encourage your child to watch and write the letters in part 1 so that they can quickly learn the sounds of the alphabet letters.

If you have any questions or problems relating to your child's learning of English, you are welcome to email me at any time.

Kind regards,
Mrs. Vaughan

随着现代信息技术的发展，书面交流除了信函和电邮之外，教师还可以用微信或其他方便的通讯工具与家长联络。No matter what format you use, letters, emails or phone calls are all allowing you to communicate and express your feelings and emotions. Depending on your communication skills, the recipient should understand you after receiving your message and you will be well on your way to developing a positive relationship with your child's parents.

Written Communication 2: Teaching Materials That Communicate–Poems, Songs and Stories

第五章中介绍了档案袋，档案袋里主要是学生的作品或学习成果。教学结束后，学生可以把学习资料或成果带回家，家长就可以更加直观、明确地掌握学生在学校的学习情况，更加便于家长及时参与到学生的学习中。Taking home poems, songs and stories for children to share

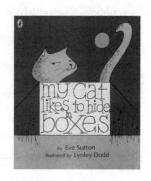

with their parents and sending emails about these or photos being posted on a blog, keeps the parents informed and involved in their child's learning.

比如，以第一章Lesson Plan 4为例，学生在学校学习了*My Cat Likes to Hide in Boxes*，课后让学生把诗歌带回家，让家长了解学校所学的内容。

同样，Lesson Plan 1中的果冻歌也是学生们喜欢的。很多学生回家后马上分享给家人，并乐此不疲。

Written Communication 3:

Table 6: Exchange Systems Help Communities

Name: _____

Exchange Systems Help Communities

How We Organize Ourselves'
ESL Vocabulary

Find out how to write the word in your home language. Then draw a picture to match the word.

English	Meaning	Picture	Home Language
exchange	to swap or trade		
systems	a set way of doing things		
benefit	help, support or assist		
community	a group of people who live together		

Find out how to say and write the central idea sentence in your home language. **Exchange systems help communities.**

_____

_____

_____

_____

_____

_____

_____

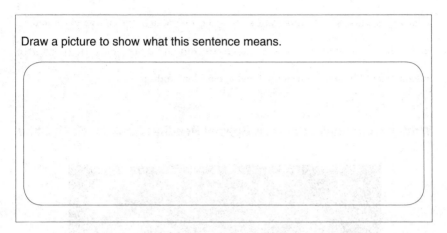

Draw a picture to show what this sentence means.

Table 6，是利用图画和母语来帮助学生识记单词的有效方法。这个方法不仅能帮助学生记忆词汇，使用母语，还因为有了父母的参与，增加了亲子互动和情感交流。

As children begin to centre their learning around a new topic, I often develop a vocabulary sheet, like in table 6, using important words and conceptual ideas which the students will need to learn in order to expand their understanding.

As I introduce this worksheet to the students, I engage them in trying to explain some of the vocabulary and drawing some little pictures for them to copy. This discussion can lead to them suggesting how to say and even write the word in their home language. Then I ask them to take the sheet home to check with their parents as to whether what they have written in their home language is correct.

为了保证并增加教学效果，我还会写封电邮给家长，让他们知晓他们的孩子会带着单词工作表回家并请他们协助完成。In the email I stress to them the importance of the discussion with their child, rather than just doing it for them. This is very important as it is the interaction and active participation that will assist their child's language development, not only their English advancement but also their home language understanding.

Written Communication 4: A Special Reading Book for Each Child

在过去的教学过程中，我会把学生们在课堂教学中用过的素材一一累积起来，日积月累，他们每个人都有了一本小册子。这有点类似于前文中提及的档案袋，但还是有所不同，这是他们的资源库和成长手记。

This book contains a growing collection of poems, songs and stories, which we have used in our lessons. It may begin with the alphabet song and the days of the week. As we learn a new poem or read a story, I put copy of it into these booklets for the children to take home to share with their parents. Sometimes it could be a story map of a well-known story, like "The Little Red Hen". Another time it may be a recipe for making gingerbread men or it could be a cloze activity sheet relating to a recent excursion that the children went on.

Besides being a record of their learning, these booklets provide the parents with an insight into their learning and a springboard for discussions to further develop the connection between their home languages and their English journeys.

2. 口头交流 Oral Communication

Story 15 : Fluent in Reading but Lacking Understanding

Imagine a child reads fluently in English but, when asked to retell the story, he makes up the story or adds entirely different details. Upon further questioning about the story, his answers clearly show a lack of understanding. Is this a language issue or is a bigger learning problem? In this instance, I called the parent in for an interview and carefully explained the situation to her. Then I suggested that she reads a book with her child in their home language, asking the child to retell the story and then ask probing questions about it to determine his understanding.

Would there need to be a follow up meeting? In this case, a further meeting was arranged a few weeks later. The child was exhibiting similar problems in their home language. Therefore, the problem was not just a language learning issue but a more general learning difficulty.

Always be careful to report back to the parents any improvement in the child's academic or social behaviour. They deserve to know what is occurring and will worry, perhaps unduly, if you fail to follow up. If the problem or learning difficulty is ongoing, you will need to continue the dialogue with the parents, walking with them along the road ahead with their child, until they are safely in the hands of other professionals.

必要的时候，一定要和家长面对面沟通。以上案例中提到的理解力问题并不一定具有普遍性，但是遇到类似的问题时，还是要坦诚地本着对孩子负责的精神与家长做好沟通。最重要的是，一定要让家长知道你关心他们的孩子。学生的福祉就是你最大的关注。（ *Most of all, let parents know that you care about their child. His welfare is your paramount concern.* ）

3. 正确表达 Communicate in a Right Way

人人都需要赞美，据说植物经过赞美也会意气风发、生机盎然，更别说人了。学生也是如此。可问题是，日常生活中的我们常常没有正确地赞美人。要想让赞美更加有效，就得好好学一学方法与技巧。

Everyone needs compliments. It is said that even plants thrive more upon being praised; it is just as true for people. But for praise to be most effective in changing behaviour, people must learn to praise correctly in daily life.

① 正确表扬 Praise For a Purpose

Story 16 : Is "You're Terrific" Universal?

"Tony, good job!"

"Tony, you are terrific!"

"Tony, you are a quick learner, and you are so smart!"

Yes, Tony was an active, pleasant and intelligent child, both at home and school; but later on, this child stopped being active and failed to respond to challenges in both the classroom and at home. And worse than that, he sometimes dared not to solve some simple problems.

People praise children (or even each other) by saying "You're beautiful", "You're smart", "You're excellent", "You're terrific" constantly. Unfortunately, such general praise may actually at times have a detrimental effect, especially with children.

When children continually hear about these "compliments" from parents and teachers, they gradually realize that "you always say things like that, no matter what I do", or for children who don't get these compliments they can think, "I must be a dumb if I cannot learn things quickly". Instead, the praise should specifically focus on what a child has done that was excellent or terrific.

"Tony，你真棒！""Tony，你学得真快，你真聪明！"

的确，Tony是个聪明活泼的孩子，老师和家人经常这样夸他。可是后来大家慢慢发现Tony有了变化，做事情不那么积极了，甚至有些畏手畏脚。

在校区听课，在公交车上，甚至家里，你都会听到有很多人用"你好聪明""你好棒""你好漂亮"等不停地夸赞孩子或成年人。其实这种夸奖赞美并不恰当。

老师和家长也许无意，但是仔细想一下，上面话语导致的下意识思考是不是这样呢——"反正不管如何，你每次都这样说！""我要是学得不快，那我就不聪明了。"

阿黛尔与伊莱恩在她们的著作《如何说孩子才会听，怎么听孩子才肯说》（*How to Talk So Kids Will Listen and Listen So Kids Will Talk*）[1]中详细告诉了我们该如何说。其实赞美不可以笼统，比如"你好棒"。刚开始小孩子也许会接受，但是时间一长，他也会发现他无论做什么都会得到这个标准答复。他会慢慢怀疑你到底说的是真是假，最后导致的是否定你言语的诚恳态度和权威性。还有就是切忌贴标签式或判断式的赞美，比如"你真聪明"。如果前面没有铺垫，那这种赞美也属于笼统式的赞美。加上前提（学得真快）的话，听者会听出言外之意。若是不快，就是不聪明了。比较常见的赞美之辞还有"你好漂亮"。这种赞美几乎是万能型的，听得多了不仅混淆是非判断，还让人心生麻木，直至无视。只是因为赞美得不够

---

① Adele Faber & Elaine Mazlish. *How to Talk So Kids Will Listen and Listen So Kids Will Talk* [M]. London: Piccadilly Press. 2013.

正确，最关键的是因为不够诚恳。

那么，该如何正确表扬呢？总结下来对孩子的赞美应大致如下：

1. 描述性赞赏。用描述你的所见和所感来代替你的评判。"我看你在上面画了一个圈，又一个圈，还在上面涂了不同的颜色呢！这么多的圈圈好有趣呢！"而不是"你画了这么多圈圈，乱糟糟的什么意思呢？"在你描述时，孩子知道你是懂他的、尊重他的劳动的，他自然会向你展示他的意图。我们大人很多时候可能并不能体会和了解孩子童心世界的美好。

2. 具体细节处赞赏。"这幅画的颜色搭配协调得当"，而不是"这幅画真美！"要说出美在何处。

3. 总结式赞赏——驱动一颗向上的心。"我看到了你的耐心和坚持，真好！"突出孩子的优秀品质！放大和激励孩子的闪光点！

请记住，赞美孩子一定要真诚、恰到好处！可以根据孩子的年龄、能力、优秀特质进行一定的导向性的赞美（praise for a purpose）。

卡罗尔·德韦克（Carol S. Dweck）博士在她《心智模型——成功心理学》（*Mindset: The New Psychology of Success*）[1]一书中同样描述了该如何表扬孩子。作为父母、教师应该赞美孩子的坚持和努力，而非夸赞孩子聪明。而且对大多数人来说，相对于夸赞孩子成功，在孩子失败时该如何沟通更为棘手。这里我们暂且引用德韦克博士的例子来阐明一下。

九岁的伊丽莎白去参加体操比赛，她身材瘦长、柔韧灵巧、浑身是劲。她已做好十足的准备，而且她非常喜欢体操。到了赛场，伊丽莎白是第一

---

[1] Carol S. Dweck. *Mindset: The New Psychology of Success* [M]. New York: Ballantine Books. 2008.

个出场，她表现得不错，但不足以获胜。比赛结束了，她一无所获。若你是伊丽莎白的父母，你会怎么说？

1. 告诉伊丽莎白，在你眼里她是最棒的；

2. 告诉她她应该获奖，却被别人不光彩地抢走了；

3. 告诉她体操真的不是那么重要；

4. 告诉她她有这个能力，下次肯定获奖；

5. 告诉她她的确拿不到那个奖。

我们都怕伤了孩子的自尊心，所以想方设法保护孩子避免失败。这样做短期来看，或许对孩子的自尊心有益，但是从长远来看，一点也不可取。

孩子都是聪明的，他们非常清楚你的言下之意。这里不再一一剖析上面五句话的言外之意。那该如何向孩子表达呢？或许选项5是个比较正确的选项，但是真的像选项5这样表达，也的确有些不够恰当。建议如下：

"伊丽莎白，我知道你很难过。原本你的期望很高，也尽可能地努力表现了自己，可还是没有赢，真的非常令人失望。你该知道，你没有获奖，也许就该是如此。因为许多优秀又有才艺的女孩子，她们勤加练习，甚至比你练得更勤快，而且练得时间又长。如果你想赢，就要比别人付出更多的勤奋和努力。"

② 恰当表达 Express Yourself Correctly

上文提到正确表扬，其实也有正确的发怒。人人都不喜欢被发泄怒气，所以鼓励大家多表扬、多激励，尽量少发怒或者不发怒。"不管是谁都能发火，这很容易。难的是向对的人，把握分寸，在合适的时刻，有恰当的理由并以正确的方式发怒"①。正所谓智者不怒，愚者不会怒。看来不管是表扬，还是发怒，都要恰当表达。

Effective communication with children (and parents) is an essential part of any teacher training program. I never knew how quickly the training worked for a young teacher until she posted her very thrilling moments on WeChat. It happened the day after a training workshop on "The Power of Language" in which I talked about "I Messages". "I just can't believe it; it worked", said Lisa.

Story 17 : "I Messages" and "You Messages"

Lisa was an enthusiastic, young teacher. When facing the hustle and bustle of managing a group of children, she sometimes felt inadequate and even seemed at a loss to know what to do. Things got even worse when a new little girl showed up in her class, who was always very active, frequently jumping here and there.

The next day after the training session about "I Messages", Lisa ushered in her class including this little girl. With no better option or method to employ, she decided to try "I Messages". Carefully, she employed this technique. After she finished her "I Messages", she had no idea what would happen next. Time seemed to stand still. She could hear her heart beating. All of the children were staring at

---

① 语出亚里士多德。转引自《非暴力沟通的觉醒》，[法]托马斯·德·昂桑布尔著，生活·读书·新知三联书店出版有限公司，北京，2019年3月出版。第170页。

her, including the new little girl and others, who had not been easily disciplined on weekdays. What were they thinking and what would they do next? Her mind went blank.

After what seemed like a very long time, the little girl came forward and gave her a big bear hug. Then the other students came and hugged her.

Lisa said that at that point she was totally surprised and her heart melted. She felt so ecstatic that she couldn't help posting to the training group on WeChat.

"By age 3, most children can understand most language they will use in ordinary conversation for the rest of their lives."[①] Children are also intelligent enough to know a heart filled with love, as long as we speak and communicate clearly and correctly.

那么，什么是"我信息"句式和"你信息"句式呢？这里必须要向简·尼尔森致敬，正是她的《正面管教》[②]给了千千万万父母和教师一种既不惩罚也不娇纵，又能有效管教孩子的方法。我们来看下面的句子：

1. 把口香糖吐出来。/ 赶紧坐下来。

2. 你为什么离开座位？

3. 你应该做得更好。

4. 你要是不排队，我就让你在这儿站一整天。

---

① B. L. White. *The First Three Years of Life*. New York: Simon and Schuster. 1995.
② https://www.positivediscipline.com/Jane Nelsen, Cheryl Erwin, Ann Duffy Roslyn. *Positive Discipline for Preschoolers* [M]. New York: Three Rivers Press. 2007. Jane Nelsen, Lynn Lott. *Positive Discipline for Teenagers* [M]. Harmony. 2014.

5. 如果我是你，我会回去学习。

6. 惹麻烦的总是你。

7. 你那样做目的就是引起关注。

8. 你今天的行为简直太不像话了。

9. 你头脑很聪明，可以做一名好学生。你只要努力就会做的很棒。

10. 我希望你长大后当老师，有一百个像你一样的学生。

从上面这些句子中，你会发现都有一个明确的"你"，即使是第一句的祈使句（下命令），也是隐藏着明确的"你"。如果仔细看下来有点专门针对"你"的感觉，言语中有"命令、指责、讥讽"等意味。这些都属于不被人接纳式的语言。不被人接纳的语言一般有命令、控制、指挥、警告、威胁、说教（总是说"应该"、"必须"）、判断、批评、不认可、指责、谩骂、归类、嘲笑等等。其实，暂且不说是孩子，就是作为成年人的我们，若是别人对我们这样说话，我们也会不高兴、不接纳。

那么，"我信息"又是如何呢？正确的"我信息"句式，是以我为主，客观描述自己所见（"你"的行为），然后谈（受"你"的行为的影响）自己的所感，之所以这样所感，是因为"你"的行为而导致。"我信息"句式表达的是主动担负起自我责任的信息。该句式中的信息有三要素：行为、影响、感受（*For example, "I feel _____ about _____, and I wish _____" formula*）。例如：

1. 我发现纸张散落在教室地板时（没有批评的陈述），任何人的话我都听不清了……（实质而具体的影响）

2. 当你没有做家庭作业时（行为描述），我得花更多的时间和精力来教这堂课（实质影响），我感到沮丧。

3. 教室里很吵时（行为描述），我上课就被干扰了（实质影响），我不得不用更大的声音（实质影响），我心里很无奈又很伤心（感受）。

4. I feel sad（感受）when you were late for school（行为描述），and I wish I could help you.

"当你在那里蹦蹦跳跳（行为），其他同学也被干扰和吵到了（影响），我也被吵到了（影响），你们学东西也学不好（影响），我不得不每次都停下来（影响），我真的很难过（感受）。"Lisa老师尝试性的一句话，居然让孩子们理解了她的境况，那一刻的她感受到了孩子们的理解与共鸣。

正面管教提出了五个标准（five criteria for positive discipline）：

A. Kind and firm;

B. Belonging and significance;

C. Tools work long term;

D. Valuable social and life skills;

E. Children develop a sense that they are capable.

沟通是门大学问，值得我们不断地学习和实践。了解孩子，也让孩子了解我们。与孩子"共情"，善用"我信息"句式，能更有效地教学。

4. 换位思考 Empathy

Story 18 : A Quarrel with the Supervisor

Lisa wanted to conduct an open class on a particular Saturday, so she reported to Maria, the grade supervisor. Maria complained that Lisa should have done this much earlier, because she had not had enough time to prepare her introductory welcome speech for the parents, even though a PPT was already organized. Lisa thought that she was not the one who should be blamed, because it was a supervisor's duty to know the schedule or arrangement of each class and give a welcome and introductory speech to the parents whenever needed. You can guess the result; Lisa and Maria had a quarrel that day.

Something unpleasant always happens in our lives. You never know when and what it is about before or even sometimes after it happens.

When Lisa recalled that event, she thought it would have been much better if she knew how to give that welcome and introductory speech based on the prepared PPT. Also, she could have informed Maria a little bit earlier. Actually, it would not have been easy for her supervisor to handle so many welcome and introductory speeches every week. At least, she could have shown a little more empathy.

She talked with Maria later on and said "Sorry". Maria also apologized for her reckless, bossy words.

领导者领导的是人心，管理者管理的是事务。无论是作为领导、管理者还是员工下属，都需要换位思考。如果能够做到换位思考，就会多一份对另一方的理解和宽容。Communicating is a kind of art. It involves not only skills, but also the heart to discern the feeling and emotions of others. This includes how to show empathy to your supervisor, just as we show empathy to our students.

换位思考，其实就是很多人说的共情、同理心。根据维基百科："Empathy is the capacity to understand or feel what another person is experiencing from within their frame of reference, that is, the capacity to place oneself in another's position." When people show their empathy, they attempt to understand the other person's feelings, thoughts and situations from their viewpoint rather than from their own perspective.[1]

人们都知道换位思考，但是做到并不容易。这个故事告诉我们，沟通时要注意换位思考，只有设身处地从别人的角度出发，达到共情，在沟通时才自然而然会换个措词交流，效果自然也完全不同。因为"懂你"、"理解"，才有古时的"士为知己者死"，可见共情是多么重要。很多时候，在对待上级或领导时，多一份理解，自己的视野和格局会变大，考虑问题也会越发全面。时间愈久，你对教学管理的理解也会愈深。试想，哪个领导会不赏识这样的人呢？！

---

[1] https://en.wikipedia.org/wiki/Empathy

5. 心理效应 Known Effects

① 人才的培养——木桶效应 Liebig's Law of the Minimum

木桶效应Barrel effect又称木桶原理wooden bucket theory，很多人认为是由美国管理学家彼得提出，但笔者以为是后人根据Liebig law of the minimum（Carl Sprengel, Justus von Liebig）发展而来的，因为Liebig用木桶形象地展示了该效应。当然也有很多人批评该效应，我们认为这个理论有其合理性。木桶效应说的是一个木桶能盛多少水并不取决于整个木桶的高度，而是取决于木桶上最短的那块短板（或者取决于某块木板上最靠桶底的那个破洞），所以木桶效应又被称为短板理论。学生的各学科犹如木桶上的各块木板，如果出现明显的短板（偏科），其整体上的素质或表现就会受到极大的影响。

A bucket consists of many pieces of wood. If the boards that make up the bucket are of different lengths, the maximum capacity of the bucket does not depend on long boards, but on the shortest board.

所以，作为教师和家长，如果学生出现某方面明显的短板或偏科，要及时提醒并帮助孩子，补齐短板，以免影响孩子的整体素质或表现。

木桶效应或短板理论对孩子早期教育的全面发展有重要的启示作用，同时也契合工业时代的职业发展需要。但在互联网时代，人们愈发重视长板，强调天赋优势的重要性。比如，公司需要有自己的长板，形成自己的"核心竞争力"，才可以打败竞争对手。因此，为了实现一个"完整的桶"的管理方，会通过合作，把其他短板补齐，强强联合，各自舍去自身短板，发挥各自的长板，形成合力和最强优势。

所以，除了尽可能在学业起始阶段提醒并帮助孩子补齐短板外，也要注意培养孩子的兴趣，发现并帮助孩子发挥其天赋优势，通才固然重要，但是未来每个人最终都是在发挥自己的长板。

② 心理暗示的力量——罗森塔尔效应 Rosenthal Effect / 皮格马利翁效应 Pygmalion Effect

美国著名心理学家罗伯特·罗森塔尔（Robert Rosenthal）通过给学生所谓的聪明鼠、笨拙鼠（其实两者都是一种老鼠）进行迷宫实验，得出聪明鼠比笨拙鼠犯错误更少的结论。随后他又到一所小学，在学生中进行了一次未来发展测试，选出了所谓的"优异"的学生（其实就是给学生贴了"优异"或"一般"的标签）并通知有关老师。八个月后，他再次进行测试，结果发现那些所谓的"优异"学生不仅成绩进步显著，在其他各方面也有显著进步。这就是后来著名的罗森塔尔效应。

古希腊神话中塞浦路斯国王皮格马利翁对一尊少女塑像产生了爱慕之情，他强烈的爱慕最终使少女雕像变为真人，两人相爱结合。因此人们又把罗森塔尔效应称为皮格马利翁效应。

罗森塔尔效应给教师和家长的启示不言而喻。心理暗示对孩童的成长有着神奇的激励作用。一个正面积极激励的眼神和表情对孩童的作用超出我们成年人的想象；同样，一副消极怀疑甚至蔑视的神情对孩子也会有极大的消极影响。笔者曾经问过许多大学生，即使过去很多年，他们仍不会忘记父母甚至老师曾经伤害过他们的"恶言恶语"，当然那些曾经激励感动他们的话语他们也记忆犹新。正面积极和负面消极的心理暗示与正面积极和负面消极的话语一样，都会对人产生巨大的积极或消极的影响。

贴标签效应也有着罗森塔尔效应般的"暗示效应"。二战期间，由于兵力不足，美国政府动员监狱犯人上战场。在培训期间，心理学家没有对犯人士兵过多说教，而是强调犯人们每周都给亲人写一封信。信的内容由心理学家统一拟定，主要是叙述自己表现得如何之好。三个月后犯人们奔赴战场，心理学家又要犯人们在信中写自己如何听从指挥、奋勇杀敌等。结果，这批犯人一如他们在信中所述，在战场中令行禁止，表现勇猛。

所以，贴标签效应告诉我们，面对学生，要想方设法给学生积极的心理暗示，善用正面积极的激励性话语，多贴正向的标签。

③ 过犹不及、物极必反的超限效应 Overteaching[1]

俄国作家克雷洛夫写过一篇名为《杰米扬的汤》的故事[2]：有一天，一个朋友远道来访，杰米扬亲自下厨，做了一大盆鲜美的鱼汤来招待。朋友喝了第一碗，感到很满意。于是，杰米扬劝他喝第二碗。第二碗下肚，朋友有点嫌多了，可杰米扬没有觉察，仍然一个劲地"劝汤"。朋友无法忍受这种盛情，借故离去。这种由于刺激过多、过强和作用时间过久而引发的逆反的心理现象就是超限效应。超限效应有些类似于我们熟知的过犹

---

[1] Robert K. Noyd. *Applying Aristotle's golden mean to the classroom: Balancing underteaching and overteaching* [J]. Teaching Matters. P4-6. 2005.
[2] 转引自崔世英，警惕教育教学中的"超限效应"，《辽宁教育》[J]. 2018年24期。

不及[1]和物极必反。

据说超限效应源于美国著名作家马克·吐温。马克·吐温在教堂听牧师演讲，被其声情并茂的演讲打动，决定捐款；过了十几分钟，牧师还没有讲完，他有些不耐烦，决定只捐一部分钱；又过了一段时间，牧师还在讲个不停，他决定不捐了。最终等到牧师结束其冗长的演讲时，他实在有些过于气愤，不仅没有捐钱，还从盘子里拿走了几美元。

在家庭教育中，超限效应常常发生，尤其出现在父母中喋喋不休的那一方和孩子之间。比如，一些好心的长辈常常哀叹自己的一片好心被当成驴肝肺，却不知自己的好心恰恰是被自己的喋喋不休给破坏成了驴肝肺，这就是超限效应的典型表现。这也是为什么那些常常滔滔不绝教训孩子的长辈发号施令好像并不起作用，而那些讲话并不多的父母每次说话都比较有分量、有影响起作用的原因。

在孩子某件事做得不够好（其实大多数时候已经很好了）时，父亲或母亲会揪住不放，然后开始一次又一次喋喋不休的教训，不仅没有起作用，反而引发亲子之间的关系紧张甚至造成矛盾，放大了孩子失败的标签与阴影，致使孩子从原本的不太在意变成很在意，甚至变得很不耐烦进而导致"我偏要这样"和"破罐子破摔"等现象。

因此，作为教师和家长，劝解孩子时，切忌喋喋不休，切忌一味说教不绝于耳。言简意赅，对孩子给予包容理解更能激励他们的上进心。对待孩子，要多学习运用"南风效应 / 法则"。

---

[1]《论语·先进》：子贡问："师与商也孰贤？"子曰："师也过，商也不及。"曰："然则师愈与？"子曰："过犹不及。"

④ 良言一句三冬暖的南风效应 South Wind Law

南风效应来源于法国作家拉冯丹的寓言故事。北风与南风打赌比赛，看谁能让行人把身上的大衣脱掉。北风寒风刺骨不但没有让人把大衣脱下来，人们反而把大衣裹得更紧了；而南风只是暖风徐动，行人顿觉温暖如春，于是解开衣扣，脱掉了大衣。很显然，南风大胜。这就是"南风法则"，又称"南风效应"或"温暖法则"。

所以，在教育学生时，用恐吓或更极端的"北风"教育方式不仅不可取，还会起到反作用；而运用"南风"，可以顺应学生真实需求，让他感觉到老师或爸妈对他的关心爱护，更容易激发他内在的驱动力从而积极向上。

前文的故事17，就体现了"语言的力量"。培训后的第二天，有位教师在微信群里兴奋地说，她主动尝试运用了"我信息"句式的沟通方式，效果超出她的想象。从另一个角度来说，亦有点像南风法则。一味地强调规则，不仅没有起到正向作用，反而有可能起了反作用；而好话一句三冬暖，受到老师的感染，学生们也会理解老师，主动放弃不良学习行为。

⑤ 激励应恰当——德西效应 Self-Determination Theory[1]

美国著名心理学家爱德华·德西（E. L. Deci）曾经做过一个著名的实验。他让大学生去做一些有趣的智力难题。第一阶段，所有人都没有奖励；第二阶段，把大学生分为两组，一组有奖励，一组没有奖励；第三阶段为大学生想做什么就做什么的休息时间。实验发现，第三阶段，无奖励组的

---

[1] https://selfdeterminationtheory.org/theory/

学生比奖励组的学生花更多的时间去解题，而奖励组解题的兴趣减少了很多。实验表明，在有内在激励（愉悦等）的情况下给予外在奖励（报酬等），反而会减少这项活动对参与者的兴趣或吸引力。这种规律就是"德西效应"。

所以，作为教师和家长，给孩童的激励要适宜。孩子没有内在的动力时，可以给些外部激励，以刺激其进步；若孩子已有些许内在的动力（比如兴趣，哪怕只是一点点），应尽力去激发其内在的驱动力，这样的动力才能持久，而不要一味给予其外部奖励，这样的奖励方式会蚕食孩子的内在动力，进而导致兴趣下降，学习目标偏离。

很多隔代祖父母辈的老人为了鼓励孩子，有时候许以重诺，买这买那，甚至吃完饭都有奖励，考试考百分奖励，考进前多少名都有奖励。久而久之，孩子的学习或做事的动力变成外部的物质刺激，逐渐丧失了内在动力，结果后期因动力不足，反而懈怠下来。

⑥ 批评的正确姿势——增减效应 Gain-Loss Effect[①]

很多人在日常生活和工作中常常先表扬，然后再提些美中不足的批评和建议。其实研究显示，人们会越来越喜欢那些对他们的喜爱不断增加的人，最不喜欢那些对他们的喜爱不断减少的人。荷兰哲学家Baruch Spinoza（1632—1677）最先提出这一观点，之后美国社会心理学家阿伦森（Elliot Aronson）通过实验证明了这一点，并把这种现象称为"增减效应"。"增减效应"实验还证明：先批评后表扬比先表扬后批评的效果好，甚至

---

① https://www.oxfordreference.com/view/10.1093/oi/authority.20110803095840471

比一直表扬的效果还好。许多售货员掌握并学会了这一点，他们在给顾客称东西时，总是先放少一点，然后再慢慢地一点一点往里添加，而不是先多装些，最后再从大盘里拿出来。

所以，在评价孩子甚至是在批评孩子时，教师和家长不妨试一试"增减效应"，先给孩子提一些小的批评和建议，然后再适当给予表扬和鼓励。孩子需要表扬，但是表扬也需要正确的方式方法。请参阅本书前文关于如何正确表扬的内容。

⑦ 倾听，让孩子的情绪得以宣泄——霍桑效应 Hawthorne Effect[1]

霍桑效应（The Hawthorne Effect）又称观察者效应（also referred to as the observer effect or viewing effect）。美国芝加哥郊外的霍桑工厂娱乐设施齐全，医疗和养老制度健全，但是工人们情绪依然不高，生产情况也不理想。后来心理学家做了一个实验，专家找每个工人进行个别谈话。专家耐心倾听工人的各种不满、牢骚和意见，及时安抚他们的负面情绪。实验证明，这样的谈话使得工厂产值大幅提高。

霍桑效应给我们的启示是：作为教师或父母一定要挤出时间来同孩子谈心，倾听他们的困惑、烦恼甚至是不满。这非常符合成功沟通的三步骤：倾听、交流、共同寻找最佳解决方案。通过让孩子诉说，努力达到共情，让孩子负面情绪得以宣泄，他们就会感到被理解，心情会变得轻松、舒畅。这样，他们在学习中就会放下包袱，安心努力，也会变得愈加自信。

---

[1] https://www.aqr.org.uk/glossary/hawthorne-effect

故事19就是教师发挥霍桑效应，让孩子诉说，教师认真倾听，弄清熊孩子无端制造事端的缘由，然后晓之以理进行交流劝解，共同找到最佳解决方案，从而解决问题的案例。

Story 19 : Pushing Fisted Knuckles into the Head of a Student

Into my Grade Two EAL class at an international school in China, a newly arrived student from Korea came. He had very limited English and was quite angry that his parents had moved him from his home country.

He particularly expressed his anger during the mandatory Chinese lessons. I was fortunate in that he preferred to learn English. Nevertheless, even in my classroom, his displeasure was palpable.

One morning, he walked into the room after the other children had sat down and as he passed a classmate from Taiwan, he pushed his fisted knuckles into the top of this unsuspecting student.

The poor victim cried out in pain. I quickly went to his aid, organizing for some ice to be applied to his head.

Next, I had to confront the culprit about why he had done this. With much wisdom, I made him face the consequences, but at the same time, I needed to address the root cause of his behaviour - his emotional feelings of the loss of all that was familiar in the move from his home country.

Over time, this student became a happy and useful member to the school community.

⑧ 教育孩子无小事——蝴蝶效应 The Butterfly Effect

气象学家洛伦兹（Edward Lorenz）认为，一只南美洲亚马逊河流域热带雨林中的蝴蝶偶然扇动了几下翅膀，就有可能引起美国德州两周后的一场龙卷风。其原理是：蝴蝶翅膀的运动，导致身边空气气流发生变化，而这微弱气流又会引起四周空气系统或其他系统相应的变化，由此引起连锁反应，最终导致其他系统的大变化，最后导致龙卷风的形成。

蝴蝶效应告诉我们，在我们看来非常小的事情，有可能会引发孩子巨大的反应。事实上也的确如此，询问成年人小时候什么事情对他们有着比较大的影响时，答案往往会出乎他们父母的意料，很多父母会说没有想到，甚至都已经忘却了那件事。有时候，父母或老师一个小小的言行举动有可能就会在孩子幼小的心灵埋下一颗种子。

⑨ "动之以情，晓之以理"，不妨试试"得寸进尺效应"Foot-in-the-door Technique

得寸进尺效应（又称"登门槛效应"Foot-in-the-door Technique）指的是，一个人一旦接受了他人的某个小小请求，为了避免认知上的矛盾，或者想留给他人前后一致的印象，会接受更大的要求。这种要求犹如登台阶，一阶一阶，不经意就会走过好几个台阶。美国社会心理学家弗里德曼与福雷瑟（Johnathan Freedman and Scott Fraser）通过实验也证实了这一理论。

许多骗子行骗老人孩童很多时候就使用了类似"得寸进尺效应"的方法。比如通知某人高中巨奖，先是恭喜贺喜一堆好话，然后要求被骗人付非常少的一点手续费，被骗人想想这么少，又是手续费，于是就支付了。

然后行骗人再次要求支付一点点，并通过各种理由把数额一点点变大，等到被骗人意识到不正常时，已经支付了很多，走了好几个台阶了。对此类骗局的研究表明，被骗人一旦支付了很少的第一笔钱，就会自动走几个台阶支付后面的几笔钱。有受骗人甚至持续走了无数台阶，被骗走大量钱款。

登门槛效应正是迎合了人们的心理反应，所以才会让人不自觉接受对方的要求。对父母或教师来说，如果要劝说孩童接受一个比较大的计划，不妨借鉴一下登门槛效应，也就是先提出一个小小的要求，而不是提出一个很高的要求。当孩童达到这个要求时再提出更高的要求，那样孩童会比较容易接受并力求达到。沟通交流中会说话永远是艺术，是智慧。

⑩ 激发好奇心——潘多拉效应 The Pandora Effect

古希腊神话中宙斯把一个盒子交给了潘多拉，告诉她千万不能打开。潘多拉越想越好奇，禁不住打开了盒子。心理学家把这种"不禁不为，愈禁愈为"的现象称之为"潘多拉效应"（又称"禁果效应"）。潘多拉效应其实就是好奇心和逆反心理在作祟。智慧型的教师和父母都会利用潘多拉效应来教育孩子。

作为教师和父母，可以充分利用孩子们的好奇心，发挥潘多拉效应在教学中的巨大作用。特别重要的是，一定要首先诱发孩子们的好奇心，激发他们的兴趣。探究式教学法就很好地发挥了潘多拉效应。

小结、反思与练习
Summary, Reflection and Practice

☐ 每个孩子都是爸妈手心里的宝，珍惜并包容孩子的所有，包括孩子们的弱点；

Children are the apple of their parents' eyes, cherished above all others and their most vulnerable point.

☐ 要与孩子们建立积极正向的关系；Build up a positive relationship with them.

☐ 坦诚以待，讲真话实话；Be honest. Speak the truth in love.

☐ 学生所需为第一要务；Always put the needs of the student foremost.

☐ 为孩子们清晰地演示每一个步骤；Give clear steps to follow.

☐ 在采取进一步行动前，永远不要让问题升级！永远把问题消灭在萌芽期；

Don't allow the problem to escalate till action is taken. Nip it in the bud.

☐ 沟通时多讲讲孩子的进步和好的事情，不讲或少讲孩子的不良行为。

Communicate improvements & good things, not just bad behaviour.

美国著名积极心理学家洛萨达（Marcial Losada）发现，幸福夫妻的对话中，积极与消极的比例是5：1。也就是说，说一句伤害人的话，要用至少五句话去弥补。他还曾提出过一个命题，说一个人积极向上的情绪是由积极情绪和消极情绪综合而成。其中的比例大致是17：6，除出来的值约为2.9013，被称作心理学的魔力数值。有研究显示，高绩效团队的正负交流沟通也趋向洛萨达比例，达5.6，接近6；而中等绩效团队大致1.9，低业绩团队仅为0.36。幸福夫妻正负交流比例达5.1，而离婚夫妻仅为0.77。因此，作为教师或家长，在与孩子正负交流沟通时，一定要注意比例，多使用正向积极的话语。

要达到良好的沟通和交流首先要学会倾听，其次是正确的表达，最后与孩子达成共识共同解决问题。

交流沟通永远非常重要！

Most important of all, as a teacher, let parents know that you care about their child. His welfare is your paramount concern.

小结 Your summary

1. _____

_____

2. _____

_____

3. _____

_____

反思 Reflection

1. One of the parents ...

2. Three things I should always keep in my mind when I talk to ...

3. I need to ...

练习 Practice

1.

2.

3.

教研团队练习 Group Discussion：

1.分组讨论教学准备（Discuss）

2.分组进行案例分享（Share）

3.分组开展讨论应用（Apply）

锦 囊 篇
Tips for Teaching

高效能教师具备很多特质，本章节加以提炼，总结出11个教学锦囊。

1. 爱与尊重 Love and Respect

不得不再次强调这两点，因为这是一切的根基和源泉。

学外语真的不是件简单的事儿，但是如果我们在教室能够展现我们对学生深深的爱和尊重，相信随后对于学习效果的作用会事半功倍。学习者学习新事物时会感觉舒适，用他们不同的表达方式或语言表达他们的想法，犯错误时也不必担心他们的老师会嘲笑或贬低他们，而是会用一种爱的方式支持他们，给他们示范正确的方式。

Learning another language is never easy but if the teacher shows a deep love and respect for the student, the subsequent learning will always be more effective. The learner will feel safe to try new things, express their thoughts in this different language, and make mistakes knowing that their teacher will not laugh at them or denigrate them but support them in a loving way and show them the correct way. This risk-taking is an integral part of any successful learning and it will only happen when a student feels loved and supported.

2. 营造安全且富有挑战性的好学环境 Set a Safe, Studious, yet Challenging Environment

高效能教师会建立一个安全、好学、富有挑战性的课堂学习环境。

高效能教师能创造出让学生感到身心安全的环境，在这里，学生允许犯错，因此进行新的学习总是会受到鼓励和支持。能够感受到来自教师的深深的爱和理解，而不是被训斥，甚至在教室受到恐吓。高效能教师要与学生共情，并愿意竭尽所能去帮助他们。

这种充满了爱的氛围和环境源于教师有强烈的欲望帮助和引导学生，从而让他们实现他们的潜能。每一个教师都渴望能够帮助学生，并为此而扮演服务的角色，竭尽全力来帮助学生发展他们的技能。这种全心全意服务的工作态度应该贯穿于他日复一日的工作；不是成为学生的受气包，而是应成为学生们的榜样，把学生的福祉放在第一位。

An effective teacher creates an emotional safety net where mistakes can happen and subsequent new learning can be supported. A student who senses the deep loving understanding of a teacher, is more likely to take risks, than one who is being dominated and even terrorized in a classroom. A teacher, who is truly able to empathize with his students, will surely be able to help them.

This loving environment springs from a teacher's passionate desire to help and guide the students to reach their potential. While the teacher has been invested with authority, the desire to help the students in his care puts him in the role of a servant who will expend every ounce of energy to help his pupils develop their skills. This meek, servant attitude should permeate all his day-to-day actions; not making him a doormat for the students but rather an example of a hard-working, focused teacher with the students' welfare uppermost in his mind.

3. 和睦相处 Be Friendly and Approachable

高效能教师会建立与学生和睦相处的友好关系。

你是否还记得你的老师毫无表情的脸、冷漠的眼神，若发现你讲话恨不得马上关你两个小时的禁闭。你肯定不喜欢这样的老师。而那些对你总是友好，甚至会开玩笑的老师，你真是喜欢不已。不要漠然冷对甚至是恫吓你的学生，哪怕是用你毫无生机的面部表情。看到学生时你可以主动微笑示意打招呼。友善地对待学生吧！因为没有人喜欢古板、面沉似水的老家伙。

Do you remember the kind of teacher who always put that poker face on, gave you that death stare, caught you talking in class and sent you to a two-hour detention just because they felt like it? I think we all do. As much as we used to dislike that teacher, he / she often had a friendly, joking side we were glad to see. Instead of scaring your students off the moment you appear somewhere, it would be enlightening for the students to see you wave to them in a merry-go-happy way. Reach out to them as a person. Be friendly but maintain your high expectations.

Nobody likes a boring, severe teacher.

世代相传的金科玉律中有这么一条——"待人如待己"（Love your neighbour as yourself，要如同善待自己一样善待自己的邻居），这对我们成为高效能英语教师有什么样的启发呢？

在数字时代以前，街坊邻居是一个人社交网络的重要组成部分。要怀着极大的兴趣与邻居和睦相处，尽己所能帮助他们、善待他们。这种关系是保持健康生活方式的关键。因为，当你有求于人时，你会非常乐于向邻居寻求帮助和支持，反之亦然。

今天，在很多方面，我们的学生要比我们的邻居离我们更近。我们与他们天天近距离相处，与他们互动，从而影响着他们，同时也影响着我们自己。这些学生非常谦逊地来到我们身边。他们想要或需要学点什么，而就我们而言，只能在英语语言上给他们帮助。我们可以选择利用我们的权威强迫他们、要求他们，也可以选择用一种充满爱与尊重的方式引导他们向我们学习。

The golden rule of "Love your neighbour as yourself" has been the guide for living throughout many generations both in the Eastern and Western world; but what does this mean and how does it relate to being an effective English teacher?

Before the digital age, neighbours were a very important part of a person's social network. It was in a person's best interest to get on well with his neighbour, helping them and befriending them as much as possible. This relationship was often seen as pivotal in keeping a healthy lifestyle because, when you had a particular need, you felt comfortable asking that neighbour for help and support and vice versa.

In many ways, our students are closer to us than our neighbours in today's society. We are close by them day by day, interacting with them in ways that often impact them as well as ourselves.

These students come to us from a position of humility. They want or need to learn something, in our case, the English language which we are able to give to them. We could choose to use our authority to impose strict commands upon them or we can choose to lead them in a loving and respectful way in order to learn from us.

4. 设置合理的目标 Set Reasonable but High Expectations and Goals

高效能教师会为学生树立合理的高远目标。

营造良好的学习氛围和环境，与学生和睦友善相处并不是说对学生没有要求，恰恰相反，高效能教师一定要为学生设立合理的高远目标。高效能教师会为学生设置合理目标，刚刚超出他们现在力所能及的，以便让他们充分挖掘和发展自我。也就是我们在第八章中所说的维果茨基的最近发展区。①了解学生能做什么，并请他们在力所能及的基础上再多做一点点，起初提供支持，然后逐渐减少帮助，以便让他们独立完成，这样可以看到他们技能的进步。

---

① 最近发展区（ZPD——Zone of Proximal Development）：指的是儿童独立地解决问题所决定的当前发展水平和儿童在成人指导下或与更有能力的同伴合作能达到的发展水平之间的一个区间（伍尔福克 2008:48；Vygotsky 1978:86）。Vygotsky. L. S. *Mind in society: The development of higher psychological processes*［M］. Cambridge, MA: Harvard University Press. 1978.

However, creating this atmosphere in our classrooms does not mean that we make life easy for our students. An effective teacher will set goals for her students just beyond what they can currently do, causing them to extend themselves and develop those new skills. (This is Vygotsky's so-called Zone of Proximal Development, briefly introduced in next chapter.)

Knowing what the students are capable of doing and then asking them to do that much more, will see the advancement of those skills. First, this is given with support and then gradually the assistance is withdrawn, so that they are only relying upon themselves, and not upon the teacher.

5. 娴熟的语言技能 Be Competent in Using English

娴熟的语言技能是高效能教师的关键。

爱学生，不仅拥有极力想指导他们学习的欲望，而且还了解学生能做什么，一定还要有娴熟的英语语言技能作为支撑。这种能力对一个高效能的教师是至关重要的，要给学生一杯水，教师要有一桶水。我们就是学生们可以模仿的活生生的范本。若我们自身的英语技能不足，学生就会学习我们的错误养成坏的学习习惯。因此，我们必须不断提高自我技能。花时间阅读一些好的原著，听听讲座和有声书，看看电影，或者与母语国家的人互动交流，对自己技能的提高是无法估量的。

A love for students followed by a passionate desire to guide their learning and a knowledge of what a student can do, must then be undergirded by a competent proficiency in using the English language. This competency is crucial if a teacher is to be effective. No one can teach another more than they know themselves. We are a model for our students to imitate. If our own language skills are inadequate, they will copy our mistakes and learn bad habits. Therefore, we must seek to improve our own skills.

Spend time reading well-written English books, watching movies, listening to lectures, audio books or interacting with native English speakers. These activities will prove invaluable for developing your own skills.

语言标准、语法正确、语速适度、课堂教学用语恰当、指令清晰、会沟通交流是高效能教师教学的有力保障。

① 发音标准清晰 Articulate Correctly and Clearly

Take the time to listen to yourself as you teach students. You may even need to record yourself and then play it back to yourself, so that you can reflect upon how you sound as you speak. Here are some questions to ask yourself:

Am I speaking clearly?

Do I complete my sentences before going on to another thought?

Is my voice easy to listen to?

Is it high-pitched or very low?

Do I modulate my voice with a natural rhythm or flow of sentences?

How could I make my voice easier for my students to listen to?

Many people do not open their mouths widely when they speak. While this may not matter in many daily interactions with native speakers, in order to be an effective language teacher, it is crucial that words are clearly articulated. Consonants are aspirated or modified within words, while vowel sounds are carefully pronounced. The lips and the tongue are critical instruments in sending out clear communication.

Students must be able to see and hear clearly so that they can distinguish sounds and words. When it is easy for them to do this, they will be able to analyse similarities and differences within words. There is a difference in how the words "ship" and "sheep" or "cut" and "cat" are pronounced. If students are having difficulty in knowing the difference, it could be that the teacher is not saying the words clearly. Students will need to gain practice in hearing the difference, but clear articulation is the first step in this process.

② 语法规范 Correct Grammar

Furthermore, an effective English teacher must model correct grammar even when communicating simple ideas with beginning students. In fact, I would suggest that this is the most critical time for speaking correct grammar, for it is at this stage that students are mimicking us and learning their first sentence structures. Unfortunately, the temptation is to so simplify our speech that we are using almost baby language or very poor English grammar, omitting word endings and articles. For example, a teacher could say "Please get book from bag." instead of correctly saying, "Please get the book from your bag." A beginning student may ask "Go toilet", but a wise and effective teacher will respond with "Yes, you may go to the toilet". Simple speech should never equate to poor grammar.

③ 词语恰当 Appropriate Word Selection

Story 20 : Remove Your Hats

My five-year-old students were standing in the front row of the assembly, as the whole school stood to attention at the beginning of a school day before the playing of the country's National Anthem. Loudly, the deputy principal commanded the students "Boys, remove your hats." None of my boys complied. They stood erect, showing no understanding of what had been asked.

Quickly, I went along the line whispering "Take off your hats. Boys, take off your hats." Immediately the young children obeyed. Respectfully, they listened to the playing of the National Anthem, before putting their hats back on and sitting down.

What had been the problem? The deputy principal had used a word, with which they were not familiar. Remove was not in their vocabulary at that moment in time. Of course, it soon was, as they repeated the action with the word.

这个故事告诉我们，词藻的选择也很重要。

④ 语速适度 Appropriate Speaking Rate

Hand in hand with speaking clearly to students, is for a teacher to speak at a slower pace. This is essential for beginning students as they grapple to recognize words and mentally translate them into their own linguistic context. Of course, as a student progresses he needs to hear words spoken at a normal rate; but at the beginning stage, an effective teacher will be mindful of his speaking rate and adjust it to suit his students' stage of development.

He would also continually clarify what he is saying, using simple vocabulary. The main purpose of speaking is to communicate ideas and information and an effective teacher will seek to optimize his communication by conveying his thoughts simply and clearly, always checking that students have understood.

⑤ 好好说话 Talk in a Correct, Clear, Engaging Voice

除了语音、语法、语速和使用恰当教学用语外，还要善于沟通交流，通俗来讲就是好好说话、会说话。这些都是语言技能，要不断培养练习。沟通交流在前面章节中已有论述，此处不赘言。总之，高效能教师要具有娴熟的语言技能，也要不断提高沟通交流水平。

6. 美美与共 Be Inclusive

高效能教师关注每个学生，让每个学生参与教学！

有些学生表现积极活跃，随时发表观点，有些学生言辞谨慎，需要多思考，但并不表明这些学生没有观点或者是不想发表观点。而由于课堂时间有限，很容易造成总是那些积极的同学发言或高度参与课堂教学的情况。这对有些学生来说可能意味着机会总是很少甚至没有，导致他们无法参与或者至少是无法高度参与课堂教学。

作为高效能教师，作为负责整个教学活动的人，每次仅仅让少数几个同学参与课堂教学活动显然是不成功的。因为，课堂教学绝不仅仅是为了少数几个（或许是尖子生）准备的。高效能教师会让更多的学生参与课堂活动，让更多的学生从中受益。

在前文第三章介绍教学策略和方法时，我们特别展开篇幅阐述了合作式学习教学法中的CLS，尤其是讲述了卡根博士提出的PIES四大原则：积极互赖（Positive Interdependence）、人人尽责（Individual Accountability）、均同参与（Equal Participation）、同时互动（Simultaneous Interaction）。这四大原则可以说是"美美与共 Be Inclusive"的完美注解。

7. 教学互联 Make Your Lessons Relevant

与生活内容相关联的教学内容永远受学生欢迎。

没有人愿意上一堂与他们的生活或所知所想毫无关联的课。一个好的老师倾听学生内心需求，并善于把所教内容与学生现在的生活关联起来。学生们很容易记住的绝对是那些与他们生活关联度高的教学内容，而不是仅仅从教材中剥离出来的他们一点也没有感觉的某个知识点。

Who would want to attend to, let alone remember a lesson to which they had no connection? A good teacher listens and connects the subject matter to the students' current lives. Students are more likely to remember something they can draw a connection to, rather than just another statement from a textbook that they have no idea about.

8. 自信镇定 Be Assertive and Stay Calm

① 自信者人信之。Be Assertive.

坚定自信不仅可以让自己有强烈的信心，这种强烈的信心也会赋能激励学生。学生就会对你和你的教学积聚信任。这一品质是高效能教师所必需的，因为作为教师，你必须要赢得学生对你的信任。

Being assertive not only boosts your own confidence, but also enforces a great impression on your students. They will recognise you as their leader. Students will develop a sense of trust, towards you and your teaching. This quality is especially essential, because as a teacher, you would want to first gain the trust of students.

② 永远保持镇定自若。Always Stay Calm

教师好比是一艘航行于大海上的船只的船长。航行中会遇到各种问题，在教室中也会如此。小朋友的世界五彩缤纷，没有什么是不可能发生的。正如我们书中所述，做一个不同年龄段的英语教师，永远不会有枯燥的时候。但是，即使面对问题不断的小朋友，作为高效能教师，请记住，你是唯一的一个在相对时间和空间里，面对他们并对他们负责的成年人，所以你首先要做的是保持镇定、心平气和。如果作为老师的你首先失去了清醒的头脑，那么你就把自己降低到小朋友一样的心智水平了。甚至，你有可能就恰恰中了他们的圈套，更不用说已经失去了老师应有的智慧。

9. 充分备课 Always Be Well-Prepared

备人、备物、备课。

首先要备人，也就是了解学生（Learn about students）。了解学生包括学生的人数、男女比例、年龄大小、来自何方等，最最重要的是要了解学生现有的英语水平。

其次要备物，就是要熟悉教室（Know how to use facilities）。要了解教室大小、学生桌椅、教师讲台、电子教具（含白板、显示屏、投影仪等）并会使用其中的器具。还要了解学校的远近、交通等状况，永远不要做一个迟到的老师。

最后要备课，就是要准备教学内容，包括教学资源（素材和教具等）（Plan and prepare everything needed）。了解了学生的情况，是为了因材施教，根据学生的情况制定教学计划（含长期或短期以及下节课的具体教学计划）。由此，根据自己的教学计划，搜集、整理、加工所需的教学材料（含物质的教具、教材、教学所需的教室环境创设和非物质的电子图文、PPT、音频和视频等）。然后，准备详细的课堂教学活动，设计安排好每个教学环节，包括如何组织使用恰当的教学用语。

10. 生动有趣 Always Endeavor to Make Lessons Interesting

没有哪个老师不想让自己的课生动有趣，可是很明显，这并不容易，尤其是让每节课都那么有趣。

保持互动。成年人的专注力比较久一点，小孩子的专注力可是没有那么久，那要怎么办，互动是不可少的。

教学互联。前文中提到，要把教学内容与学生的生活联系起来，这样才比较有意思。

游戏教学。这绝对是不可或缺的。有谁不爱寓教于乐的游戏呢？

善用科技。电子时代的孩子人人都有电子基因。若教室有智能白板或科技化的教学器具，请善于运用高科技，玩点好玩的。这也是备课中备物之必需。

动起来，人人参与。

不妨偶尔制造点神秘感和新奇感。在设计课程的时候可以加入一些其他的元素，比如带把吉他，扮个孩子们喜欢的小丑，邀请个神秘嘉宾，观摩某个与教学内容有关的现场等等。

11. 成长型思维 Love Learning with a Growth Mindset

作为教师，同样会经历所有职场人所遇到的困惑和迷茫，尤其是新教师，压力有可能会更大、易受伤害、极其关注别人如何看待自己、不知该如何求助、被分配了更有挑战性的任务等等，这些都有可能会让新教师陷入慌乱，稍微适应一点环境之后紧接着就是挣扎。在慌乱中挣扎难免又丢三落四，还何谈成为高效能教师。这最后的锦囊便是转换思维模式，成为一个热爱学习、具有成长型思维的人。

成长型思维模式的人，看待事物的方式和方法与定式思维的人不一样，比如面对挫折甚至是失败，成长型思维模式的人会勇于直面，认为失利甚至是失败只不过是成长学习过程的一次经历而已，不管任何时候，成长型思维模式的人想做的不是去评判或被别人的评判所左右，而是要学习成长，以及怎样才能更好地学习成长。让自己纠结于尴尬、内疚、委屈、失败，还是让自己从经历中学习和成长，高效能教师选择的是后者。

高效能教师是拥有成长型思维模式的终身学习者。

小结、反思与练习
Summary, Reflection and Practice

高效能英语教师的特质有：

☐ 爱护并尊重学生；Love and respect.

☐ 善于营造安全且富有挑战性的好学环境；Set a Safe, Studious, yet Challenging Environment.

☐ 能进行有效的语言沟通；Effective Communication.

☐ 与学生关系融洽，友善不失原则；Be Friendly and Approachable.

☐ 为学生设置合理的目标；Set Reasonable but High Expectations and Goals.

☐ 拥有娴熟的英语语言技能；Be Competent in Using English.

☐ 关注每一个学生；Be Inclusive.

☐ 教学内容与现实相联系、有意义；Make Your Lessons Relevant.

☐ 自信镇定；Be Assertive and Stay Calm.

☐ 备课充分；Always Be Well-Prepared.

☐ 课堂生动有趣；Always Endeavor to Make Lessons Interesting.

☐ 是具有成长型心智的终身学习者。Love Learning with a Growth-Mindset.

In summary, an effective English teacher with a growth mindset will love his students passionately desiring to help them by setting high expectations for them and modelling a mastery of the English language through clear, careful and grammatically correct speech.

小结 Your summary

1.

2.

3.

反思 Reflection

1. No. 1 survival tip for me is ...

2. The biggest challenge for me is ...

3. I am excited about ...

练习 Practice

1.

2.

3.

教研团队练习 Group Discussion：

1.分组讨论教学准备（Discuss）

2.分组进行案例分享（Share）

3.分组开展讨论应用（Apply）

第八章
常见问题互动问答
Q & A

在考虑结语时，脑海中浮现出几个问题，也是新教师入职培训课或一些家长常常问及的。这里略加阐述，希望对有同样问题的教师有所帮助。

1. 几个常见的术语 Helpful Basic Terms

① 外语、母语、一语、二语[①] EFL, MT, L1 and L2

外语是相对于母语而言的；母语是其族群语言，大多数情况下母语是一个人出生时就开始学习的第一语言，也是其最熟练的语言。但也有例外，有些人的母语并不熟练。一个人在习得母语之后开始学习的其他语言被称为第二语言甚至是外语。第二语言与外语是两个概念，因为有些国家的官

[①] W. Littlewood. *Foreign and Second Language Learning* [M]. Cambridge: Cambridge University Press. 1984. R. Ellis. *The Study of Second Language Acquisition* [M]. Oxford: Oxford University Press. 1994.

方语言不止一种，外语有可能是其第三种语言甚至是第四种语言。有学者认为第一语言是一个人最熟练的语言，而其他语言都是第二语言。从理论上来说，界定母语和第一语言可以用不同的标准，在此不详细赘述。

外语一定是他国的语言，不具备教育用语和社会用语的功能，学习者一般都是在教室中课堂上学习这种语言。因此，在中国，英语是被当作外语来学的，虽也有说法是把英语当做世界通用语来学，但英语毕竟不是中国的官方语言，不具备教育用语和社会用语的功能，英语对国人来说即为外语。有人把这两个概念混为一谈，对第二语言和外语不加区分，所以在应用国外学者二语习得理论时他们不假思索就拿来奉若圭臬，其实是不够负责任的。

这也是简单介绍这些基本概念的根本原因，有些教育理论和教学方法策略是基于其语言环境的，当教学的语言环境发生了改变，则运用相应教育理论而实施的教学方法和策略要做些调整甚至改变，按照当今流行的说法就是要本土化。

完全照抄照搬或囫囵吞枣式使用别人的教育理论或素材，忽略了学习者的学习语境和本土化是欠妥当之举。目前有教育机构全盘使用国外（其学习者以英语为母语）的课程体系和教学计划。这种全部拿来主义，未对其课程和教学进行适度调整或有效改编的做法是值得商榷的，这也是为什么当前上市的几家主流少儿英语机构都在进行课程研发改编的原因。

举个例子，目前全世界汉语热，按照有些机构的逻辑和做法，国外开设中文课的各类学校应把中国中小学语文教材直接引进使用为妙。但情况并非如此。再以美国WIDA（World-class Instructional Design and Assessment）

为例，WIDA意为世界级教学设计和评估。因为美国是个多元文化国家，也是个移民国家，很多母语为非英语的移民的孩子与当地出生成长的英语为母语的孩子既有不同特点也有不同的英语学习需求，WIDA专为这些母语非英语的美国中小学学生进行英语语言教学设计和英语语言能力评价。

② 学习和习得 Learning and Acquisition

语言学习是指学习者为了掌握目标语而进行的有意识的学习和研究；而习得通常指的是语言学习者通过大量接触和使用目标语而潜意识地获得该语言。不少人包括教师和家长甚至有个别学者把习得和学习混为一谈。在了解了外语、母语、一语和二语等概念的基础上，作为教师、课程研发人员、教学管理层以及家长应该了解学习和习得的不同，尤其是在语言环境上。这也是为什么有教育培训机构强调沉浸式学习，因为强调的不仅仅是其沉浸式教学方法，更在强调其语言环境的提供。但总体来说，由于英语在我国并没有大范围高频度被使用，所谓的英语习得环境也就有很大程度的局限性，只剩下教室（或者学校）和家庭的某一时段了。

一般来说第一语言习得是指在儿童的第一语言的环境中逐渐掌握该语言的过程。除非发生意外情况，正常儿童都能在第一语言环境中习得该语言（通常是其母语），所以第一语言习得又称母语习得。第二语言习得是指在第二类语言环境中的语言习得，比如中国人在美国或英国学习英语，在法国学习法语等。大多数中国人学习英语实际上主要是外语学习，很多中国人都谈不上什么外语习得，因为他们哪怕一点点的外语习得环境都没有。

沉浸式学习方法就是源于习得理论，毕竟习得的重要特征就是语境。

习得是在纯粹的或有相当规模的目标语言环境中发生的语言学习，而学习是在目标语国家之外的他国语言环境且没有一定的目标语言环境下发生的语言学习。这样比较下来，当然人人都希望习得，在语境中学习目标语。有一点要清楚的是，沉浸式只能部分地解决习得语境，而母语习得是全方位的。但从另一个角度讲，有沉浸式学习总归是好的，因为哪怕是提供一点点的语言习得环境，对孩子的学习还是有促进作用的。

很显然，语言习得比语言学习效果好。以习得为导向的教学建议是[①]：

1. 语言输入越多越好，基于意义的课堂教学越多越好；

2. 课堂教学中的互动越多越好；

3. 所有学习者的语言输出都应基于意义或交际；

4. 语言结构教学应该基于意义并与输入或交际相联系；

5. 我们应该密切关注我们对学习者的期望。

③ 最近发展区 ZPD

最近发展区原文为Zone of Proximal Development，是苏联著名教育家、心理学家、社会建构主义理论奠基人维果茨基（L. Vygotsky, 1896—1934）于20世纪30年代提出的，是其主要成果和贡献。最近发展区又被称为魔法中心（Magic Middle），介于学生已有知识和尚未有能力学习的知识之间，指的是儿童独立地解决问题所决定的当前发展水平和儿童在成人指导下或与更有能力的同伴合作能达到的发展水平之间的一个区间。他认为儿童已

---

① Bill Van Patten. *From Input to Output: A Teacher's Guide to Second Language Acquisition* [M].
北京：世界图书出版公司. 2007.

有发展水平与潜在发展水平这两种发展水平之间存在着差距。儿童已经具有的独立解决问题的能力，是其已有发展水平；儿童现在不具备，但在他人的帮助下解决问题的能力，即为潜在发展水平。教师教学应该关注的是其最近发展区，而非已有的发展水平区，只有这样才能促进儿童成长。教师关注"最近发展区"，但又不能停留于此，而是要在适应"最近发展区"的基础上，跨越到"目标发展区"，帮助学习者逐步实现由量到质的飞跃。

最近发展区（ZPD）给少儿英语教师、课程研发人员以及家长的启示是，无论在教学设计还是在教学中，或是在陪伴孩子成长的过程中，应该"因材施教"，首先了解学生已有知识水平和认知发展情况，也就是已知发展区，针对其最近发展区设计教学环节和教学内容，适度地引导并给学习者提供必要的帮助，从而实现教学效果的最大化。

④ 有效"输入"[①] Effective Input

众所周知，语言习得的过程是语言输入、输出及两者之间互动的过程。语言输入是输出的前提和基础；语言输出是输入的目的和强化。语言学家Krashen（1982）的语言输入说（Input Hypothesis）指出，在外语学习中，要使得语言习得得以发生，有必要让学习者理解的输入语言包含稍高于其现有语言能力的语言项目，这种语言输入虽稍难，但仍是生动有趣的，与话题相关的，而不是照语法特意安排的内容，学习者可以利用背景

---

① S. Krashen. *The Input Hypothesis: Issues and Implications*［M］. London: Longman. 1985. S. Krashen. *The Natural Approach: Language Acquisition in the Classroom*［M］. Oxford: Pergamon. 1983.

Bill VanPatten. *From Input to Output: A Teacher's Guide to Second Language Acquisition*［M］. 北京：世界图书出版公司. 2007.

知识、情境提示或手势语调等其他非语言的线索来理解这些语言。Krashen 认为语言习得是通过语言输入来完成的，教学的主要精力应放在为学生提供最佳的语言输入上。最佳的语言输入应具备以下特点：1）可理解性（comprehensibility）；2）既有趣又有关（interesting and relevant）；3）非语法程序安排（not grammatical sequenced）；4）要有足够的输入量（sufficient input）。

语言输出同样也很重要，Swain（1985, 1995）[1]的输出假设指出，准确得体的语言输出有以下三个功能：输出具有促进"注意"或语言提示的功能；输出有助于验证学习假设；输出具有原语言功能。也就是说，输出使得学习者尝试新的语言规则并在交际中进行调整；帮助学习者反思自己对目的语言的认识；验证输出语言的正确性和有效性，借助目标语来学习目标语。

本书之所以对"有效输入"略加阐述，除了稍微澄清这个概念本身，还有另外一个原因，那就是回答后续何时进行语言启蒙和线上线下哪个更有效的语言学习问题。笔者坚信，无论是线下传统教学还是线上网络教学以及课程设计本身，都必须要考虑有效输入，因为有效输入是教学效果的最基本保障。

---

① Merrill Swain. *Communicative Competence: Some Roles of Comprehensible Input and Output in its Second Language Acquisition*［A］. Rowley, MA: Newbury House. 1985.

　　Merrill Swain. *Three Functions of Output in Second Language Acquisition*［A］. *Principles & practice in Applied Linguistics*［C］. Oxford: Oxford University Press. 1995. P125–132.

⑤ "因材施教"[①] Personalized Teaching

"因材施教",对国人来说听起来非常自然,甚至有些熟视无睹,但这不仅是孔子教育思想和理念中最著名的教学法之一,还是迄今为止在世界上依然被广泛应用的最重要的教学法之一。现今很多学校、教育公司或机构在寻找教育思想或理论支撑时通常把目光抛向国外教育家和思想家的理论,这无可厚非,可中国历史悠久,其教育思想也同样璀璨于世界民族之林。以孔子(公元前551—公元前479)为例,孔子作为我国伟大的教育家和思想家,他"是中国第一个使学术民众化、以教育为职业的教授老儒",冯友兰认为,孔子的行为及他在中国历史上的影响与苏格拉底的行为及其在西洋历史上的影响十分相似[②]。孔子是中国古代著名的思想家、教育家,热爱教育事业,具有丰富的教学实践经验。孔子教育思想中德育方面的比较多,这里首先简介一下"因材施教,各取所长"。无论是教授成人还是孩子,任何时候都无法忽略教学三大基本要素中的学生,而备课都要包括备学生,这个备学生就是要了解当前学习者的知识水平、兴趣爱好甚至是性格特点,以便根据学习者的具体情况,进行教学设计开展教学,即"因材施教"。很显然,所有的课程设计、教学设计都要基于学生的实际情况,不了解学生,就无法实现ZPD。脱离了学生的教学设计和课程设置都将会是无源之水,无本之木。时至今日,"因材施教"依然是教育界展开教学和科研的理论基石之一,在中国知网上键入"因材施教",立即可发现相关的教学科研论文论著有六千余条。

---

① 金莉. 孔子因材施教思想对当代教师专业发展的启示 [J]. 长春师范大学学报. 2019(9).
② 孙培青. 中国教育史 [M] 上海:华东师范大学出版社. 2011.

除了"因材施教"，孔子著名的教育方法或理念还有"循循善诱"、"有教无类"和"诲人不倦"等等。"循循善诱"说的就是启发引导，可以说就是启发式教学或探究式教学的最早表述。"因材施教"即在根据学习者的知识水平和认知规律对教学目标和内容进行科学设置和教学组织过程中，运用各种教学工具、手段和方法，采用启发引导的办法进行知识传授和能力培养，使学习者主动积极地进行自我驱动学习。而"有教无类"和"诲人不倦"更是倾向于一种教育思想，在这里更像是一种职业素养——师德的标准和要求。不管学生来自何方、成绩好坏、性别身高，教师都应该平等对待，把所有学生纳入自己的教育范围，根据他们现有情况的千差万别（包括学业水平和性格迥异等各种情况），制定出适合他们的教学纲要和课程设计。这与我们前文中教学方法和教学锦囊中的相关内容如探究式教学法（Inquiry Teaching）、美美与共（Be Inclusive）等十分相似。仔细研读，读者会发现当今盛行的很多教学法与孔子的"因材施教"、"循循善诱"、"有教无类"和"诲人不倦"多有契合。

2. 语言启蒙早教 Early Childhood Language Development

① 联合国儿童基金会[①] UNICEF

联合国儿童基金会2001年度白皮书告诉我们："开始确保健全生

① https://www.unicef.org/earlychildhood/index_69851.html，本部分所引用图表均引自联合国儿童基金会网站或其2001年白皮书。

活的时间越早越好（*The best time to start ensuring a full life is as early as possible.* ）。儿童语言发展从什么时候开始呢？我们来看下图：

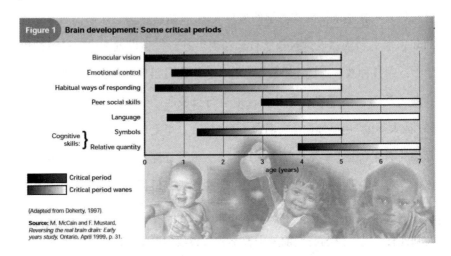

从上图可以看出儿童出生后不久就迅速进入其语言发展关键期，该关键期一直延续至7岁。可见对孩子语言的启蒙早教是越早越好，尤其不要错过孩子语言的关键期（又称敏感期、发展高峰期等）。

早期儿童发展被认为是人力资本进行的最符合成本效益原则的投资之一，因其可直接导致一个国家的可持续发展。来自发达国家和发展中国家的经济分析都不约而同得出这个结论，该结论中的主要观点是：最早投资早期教育，带给家庭、社会和国家的回报比例就最高。（*Early Childhood Development is seen as one of the most cost efficient investments in human capital which leads to a country's sustainable development. Economic analyses from the developed and developing world is converging on a set of conclusions, with the main idea being that investing in the earliest years leads to some of the highest rates of return to families, societies and countries.*）

来自芝加哥儿童与父母中心的一项研究显示，对儿童早期发展每美元投资，收益大约为7.10美元。联合国儿童基金会在2001年的世界儿童年度白皮书上指出，政府和家庭对孩子免疫、健康和教育的投入都应从零岁开始。

② 哈佛大学儿童发展研究中心[①] Center on the Developing Child at Harvard University

鉴于儿童早期发展的重要性，世界各国很多机构在儿童早期教育方面都作了大量的研究。本书仅以哈佛大学儿童发展研究中心研究成果做一列举说明。

哈佛大学儿童发展研究中心发现：大脑是随着时间的推移自下而上成长构建的，并且是从出生前开始一直到成年持续构建。先形成最简单的神经连接和技能，继而是更复杂的回路和技能。在生命的最初几年，每秒钟就形成超过一百万个新的神经连接。（*Brains are built over time, from the bottom up. The basic architecture of the brain is constructed through an ongoing process that begins before birth and continues into adulthood. Simpler neural connections and skills form first, followed by more complex circuits and skills. In the first few years of life, more than 1 million new neural connections form every second.*）这其中包括语言区的成长发展。而且大脑各区域的发展不是单一发展，而是相互支持关联成长的（*You can't have one type skill without the*

[①] https://developingchild.harvard.edu/

other to support it）。如同建造一间房子，房屋的各个部分是相互连接在一起的（*Like building a house, everything is connected*）。

家庭对儿童语言早期发展构成重要影响的另一个重要例证是有些人听说的"三岁前的3000万词汇差距"。[①]

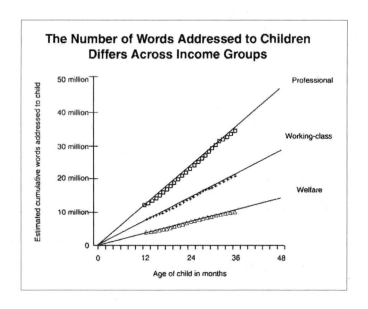

---

① https://www.aft.org/sites/default/files/periodicals/TheEarlyCatastrophe.pdf

　　研究发现：父母与孩子交谈的次数越多，孩子的词汇量增长越快，孩子在3岁及以后的智商测试得分就越高。一个有着"健谈"父母的孩子在前四年听到了4500万词汇的话，一个有着"沉默寡言"父母的孩子仅仅听了1300万词汇，从而形成了累计3000万词汇的差距。

　　有人把这个研究归功于哈佛大学，也有人说是哥伦比亚大学的研究。但确切地说是Hart & Risley[①]在1995年发表的研究成果。Hart & Risley的研究显示：贫困线以下接受社会福利的父母、蓝领父母和大学毕业的白领父母，由于父母给孩子的关注和早期教育不同的原因，他们的孩子从18个月开始，词汇量多少就有明显差别，到36个月，大学毕业白领父母的孩子的词汇量是其他两组家庭孩子词汇量的2倍至3倍。孩子本身不存在多少差异，因为婴幼儿都有吸收性心智，可是孩子父母的差异即会导致孩子词汇量的巨大差异。

　　Hart & Risley的研究不仅证明家庭环境对儿童成长发展的重要性，同时也告诉我们语言发展在儿童早期就已经显示出不同发展轨迹，而我们就是要及早开展语言教育。

③ 蒙台梭利[②] Montessori

　　记得有一次在参观一家蒙台梭利幼儿园时，见到走廊的墙壁上装饰着

---

① *The Early Catastrophe* by Betty Hart & Todd R. Risley节选自1995年出版的*Meaningful Differences in the Everyday Experiences of Young American Children*. Baltimore, MD: Brookes Publishing，2003年经作者本人同意发表在American Educator. Spring 第4至第9页。

② 陈凤兵，方红. 论蒙台梭利教育思想认识的主要误区［J］现代教育科学. 2017（6）. P128−131.
　　玛利亚·蒙台梭利. 祝东平译. 蒙台梭利早期教育法［M］北京：中国发展出版社. 2011.
　　段云波. 蒙台梭利幼儿教育法［M］北京：科学技术文献出版社. 2016.

蒙台梭利博士的照片和她的教育至理名言。其中有句话是这样的，"I hear and I forget, I see and I remember, I do and I understand"。这句话特别符合蒙台梭利的教育思想。后来有位教育名师告诉我，这话并非蒙台梭利所说，而是孔子的话，只不过是与蒙台梭利教育思想比较一致而已。后来细查，知乎给出的解释是，该句话出自孔子弟子荀子的《儒效篇》，原文是"不闻不若闻之，闻之不若见之，见之不若知之，知之不若行之。"笔者认为，之所以产生这样的误会，是因为蒙台梭利博士的教育观与荀子这番言论一致。蒙台梭利博士处处践行了这一教育理念。

蒙台梭利（1870—1952），全名为玛利亚·蒙台梭利（Maria Montessori），是意大利第一位女医学博士和女医生，蒙台梭利教育法的创始人，曾经三度获得诺贝尔和平奖提名。蒙台梭利的学术之路贯通数学、自然科学、现代语言、生物学、医学、教育哲学、普通教育学、实验心理学和教育人类学。在罗马大学附属医院担任精神病临床助理医生期间，她的工作主要是治疗智障儿童，两年后蒙台梭利总结出了两个观点：首先，创造智力需要靠手的活动；其次，要克服智力上的不足主要靠教育的手段，而不能只靠药物的治疗，或者说教育的手段比药物的治疗更有效。这两个结论引起了医学界和教育界的强烈反响。之后她作为意大利国立启智学校校长又全身心继续贯彻实践自己的教育理论思想，并大获成功。1901年，国立启智学校的智障儿童和正常儿童的考试成绩居然相差无几，这个考试结果震惊了全罗马。为了研究正常儿童，她辞去校长职位，重回罗马大学修读教育哲学、普通教育学、实验心理学和教育人类学。1907年，蒙台梭利建立了第一所早教机构——"儿童之家"。她运用自己独创的方法进行教学，教学效果惊人。蒙台梭利随后的一生都在不断从事幼儿教育的研究与实践。她先后出版了多部著作。时至今日，蒙台梭利教育已经散播到全世界110多个国家和地区。

有些教育机构甚至是家长在对蒙台梭利教育并不完全了解的情况下，断定蒙台梭利教育不适合自己的孩子，因为在他们的心目中，蒙台梭利教育只是适合于特殊的（智障）儿童。这其实是个误会或曲解，蒙台梭利博士早期的确是针对智障儿童进行的教育实践和研究，不过她从1907年起就开始了正常儿童的教育实践和研究。她的主要著作都是在其大量的教育实践研究基础上成就的。有些著作是其从事教育三四十余年之后出版的，比如《童年的秘密》（1936）、《吸收性心智》（1948）、《了解你的小孩》（1948）、《发现儿童》（1948）。也许蒙台梭利教育思想和教育法不是完美万能的，但是蒙台梭利博士的教育法的确是其通过科学的研究方法——探索研讨而成的。这一点无论是从其教学研究学术之源、教育工作手册、教育理论著作，还是从其儿童之家的精美的系列化教具中都可以看得出来。

蒙台梭利教育思想理念主要有：敏感期（the Sensitive Periods）、吸收性心智（the Absorbent Mind）、蒙台梭利教具（the Montessori Materials）和蒙台梭利教学法（the Montessori Methods）。

蒙台梭利通过对幼儿自然行为的细致、耐心、系统观察指出，"儿童在每一个特定的时期都有一种特殊的感受能力，这种感受能力促使他对环境中的某些事物很敏感，对有关事物的注意力很集中，且很有耐心，而对其他事物则置若罔闻"。蒙台梭利把儿童呈现这一现象的该关键期称之为"敏感期"。敏感期是婴幼儿遵从自然规律成长的体现，俗话说"三翻六坐七爬"，可谓明证。儿童敏感期可以分为秩序敏感期、手和口的敏感期、行为敏感期、对细微事物感兴趣的敏感期和社会性敏感期。以图1语言的发展和图2运动的发展[①]为例。

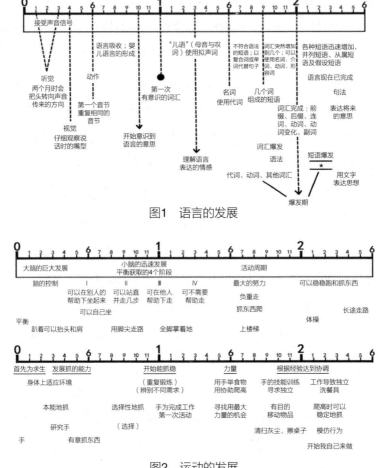

图1　语言的发展

图2　运动的发展

① 图1图2均引自段云波. 蒙台梭利幼儿教育法［M］北京：科学技术文献出版社. 2016. P69, 72.

　　语言是人类的天赋潜能。幼儿一出生就能够使用口头表达，婴幼儿早期不会说话，但是他们可以用不同的哭声来表达自己的意愿，而妈妈大多数时候也可以通过哭声来了解儿童的大致意愿。有研究表明，0~12岁是语言学习的黄金期，其实也就是语言发展的敏感期。蒙台梭利认为0~6岁是语言的敏感期，尤其是0~3岁时期对儿童语言发展具有十分重要的意义。这也是世界各地早教机构近年来愈加盛行的原因之一，同时也揭示了家长们对少儿英语愈加重视的秘密。从图1可以看出，儿童从出生时期开始的听，到六个月左右发出第一个音节，再到第一次有意识的词汇，直至2岁半左右语言爆发都是自然而然发展完成的。婴幼儿个体存在一定的差异，但是总体上基本都是遵照如此规律，英国早期教育体系（EYFS）虽然用了时间段的概念来描述，但大致发展规律也是如此。既然敏感期如约而至又如此重要，那么对这个阶段的教学、课程设计、家庭早教或护理自然而然就要遵循敏感期的发展。

　　吸收性心智（the Absorbent Mind）是蒙台梭利的又一重大发现和贡献。吸收性心智顾名思义就是指能够吸收周围环境中的知识的心智。虽然婴幼儿早期行为大多处于潜意识范畴，可是婴儿天生具有这种无意识的智慧，通过这种天赋自然而然吸收知识，这就是吸收性心智。基于孩子的敏感期和吸收性心智，蒙台梭利经过实践后研发整理了一系列的教具（the Montessori Materials）和蒙台梭利教学法（the Montessori Methods）。限于篇幅，此处不再作蒙台梭利的全面解析。丰富多彩而又精美实用的教具是蒙台梭利教育的一大亮点，与配套的蒙台梭利教育法相结合，使蒙台梭利教育走向了全世界。

综上所述，无论是蒙台梭利，还是哈佛大学儿童发展研究中心，亦或是联合国儿童基金会，都认同儿童早期教育的重要性，儿童早教越早越好。

正如我们都知道的，只要稍微给一个物体作用力，在没有任何阻力的真空情况下，该物体会一直运动下去。可是生活中的现实情况并非如此，学外语也是一样。理论上学习外语语言越早越好，可是生活中处处充满了变量因素。很多人只是关注理论上孩子语言系统发展的高峰期对孩子掌握语言的影响，却可能忽略了孩子自身认知发展，以及其本人身处的家庭、学校和社会语言习得环境对其语言发展的影响，尤其是原生家庭环境对孩子的影响。故事21"两姐妹的故事"就是一个明显的案例。

Story 21 : Two Young Sisters' Story

Many people believe that the earlier a child begins to learn a new language the easier it will be for them. Young children seem to quickly learn how to communicate with other children with little seeming effort, while an older child seems to struggle and take longer.

Two young sisters came to our Singapore School from Korea when they were aged four years old and seven years old. Neither of the girls had learnt any English before they arrived at our school. However, the older sister was able to read and write in Korean having completed two years of compulsory education.

The older sister made great progress in learning English. When discussing new conceptual vocabulary, such as barter or exchange, systems and communities, this girl could quickly explain the words in Korean to another boy who had been learning English for over a year.

In the meantime, her younger sister made much slower progress in learning to write the sounds of the English alphabet as well as high frequency words. After seven months of learning English, this younger girl could sound out some phonetically regular words and could complete a sentence with some assistance. However, the older sister was already able to write paragraphs of 100 to 150 words as she wrote her own stories.

My premise is that the older girl was conceptually more mature and literate in her mother tongue, thus allowing her to transfer her learning across to her second language.

Therefore, the best way that we can help a child to learn another language is for their home language to be well developed.

3. 线上线下学习的关键 Learning Online or Offline

孩子的学习有个关键点，那就是有效输入，而有效输入的最佳捷径就是 "你来我往式互动（serve and return interaction）"。

麻省理工大学的学者Romeo和Gabrieli研究[①]发现，与孩子对话远比丢给他们词汇对孩子大脑发展更为重要（*Study finds engaging young children in conversation is more important for brain development than "dumping words" on them*）。你来我往来来回回的交流互动可以激发孩子大脑对语言的回应

[①] http://news.mit.edu/2018/conversation-boost-childrens-brain-response-language-0214

（ *Back-and-forth exchanges boost children's brain response to language* ）。

孩子天生是个社交型学习者，需要被关注和互动。正如前文所论及的输入，要实现有效的输入，一是可理解内容，二就是要互动。

选择线上还是线下，首先看孩子的适应情况，正常来说年纪越小的时候应该选择线下，这样选择的原因是因为线下保证了和老师的互动。有人说虽然我们年龄小，但我们选择线上一对一，互动也很好。这具体得看孩子的情况，还有线上英语教师的水平。小孩子线上的课程很多，有些课程每节课也就15分钟至25分钟，之所以如此，就是因为长时间线上学习对孩子来说如果没有互动，就是煎熬。虽然说有线上互动，可那毕竟只是线上互动，远不如线下互动来得直接，比如一个拥抱。至于录播课，对年龄较小的孩子来说，其作用的确有待商榷，根本原因就是缺乏互动。无法互动，就很难达到有效输入。

我个人还是偏向小孩子线下学习，或线上线下混合式学习。即使有少儿线上课程，且不说线上课程设计和教学质量如何，家长的跟踪也是必不可少的，让孩子利用所学实现互动（使用）才能保障效果。

哈佛大学儿童发展研究中心最新研究成果——大脑强健5步互动法（5 steps for brain-building serve and return）值得借鉴。

第一步：共同关注（Step 1 Share the focus）。

当孩子关注某个物体时，老师或家长马上关注，这即为serve；关注孩子所关注的可以建立好奇心并加强与孩子的亲密关系。

第二步：支持鼓励（Step 2 Support and encourage）。

通过说出鼓励的话语 to return the sreve，如 "That's right"、"Very

good"对孩子做出回应，说出"Thank you"继续进行鼓励回应孩子的serve。面部的表情同样可以给孩子以鼓励，或者是用动作来积极回应。孩子指向某个物体时，你可以把它拿近，理解孩子并和孩子共情。

第三步：叫出名字（Step 3 Name it）。

叫出名字来，说出孩子们想说或想表达的，在大脑中产生语言（与事物的）连接。你可以叫出一个人a person、一件物体a thing、一个动作an action、一种情感a feeling的名字或者进行复杂描述，如the baby sitting in the backseat of the car，说出任何事物的名字来都可以。

第四步：轮流来（Step 4 Take turns back and forth）。

轮流来做事帮助孩子学会自控和与他人相处。等待非常重要，给孩子回应的机会。通过等待，让孩子思考出自己的想法，建立信心和独立意识。

第五步：练习结束或开始（Step 5 Practise endings and beginnings）。

孩子会示意某件事结束，然后注意力转向另外的事物。注意观察孩子开始新事务，比如说扔掉手中的一个玩具，去换了另外一个新玩具，这意味着新事务的开始。这时候回到第一步，共同关注share the focus非常重要。

跟随孩子，给孩子支持和鼓励，让他们去探索，而我们则与孩子好好交流，做好互动（serve and return）。

总之，无论是选择线上还是线下，教师能与孩子在教学期间进行互动，实现有效输入最为重要。

4. 再谈在线教学 More about Online Teaching

随着网络技术的不断发展，尤其是人工智能等技术的广泛运用，自适应学习等在线教育已成为现实。除了不受地域、空间甚至时间等局限外，其个性化学习、因材施教式的教学特点也使得在线教学独领风骚。尤其是在线下教育受交通、公共安全等因素影响时，更凸显了在线教育的优势。虽然在线教育具有诸多优势，但我们也应该看到其客观存在的弊端。下面我们对在线教学和线下教学的利弊作个简单的对比，并对在线教学提出建议。

	线下教学		在线教学		建议
	优点	弊端	优点	弊端	
教师	1）教师可随时了解并掌控学生学习状态 2）教师可及时调整教学内容、教学节奏 3）教师可巡视教学 4）互动性强且活动多元化	1）受班级规模限制，相同教学内容需要重复上课 2）若大班上课互动性差	1）在线教学班级人数规模可控可调整 2）课堂管理统计省时、省力、快捷、方便，比如签到、评分、答题 3）老师面对屏幕上课，不必大声讲话	1）教师对课堂教学掌控度减弱 2）教师在面对屏幕讲课时无法得到学生的即时反馈，无法及时调整教学节奏 3）面对屏幕上课眼睛容易疲劳 4）互动性减弱 5）对技术软件依赖性强，教学成本高 6）对教师网络技术要求高	1）熟悉并熟练使用网络直播平台和相应软件技术，善用抢答、评分、反馈等手段 2）增加课堂互动的多元化
学生	1）注意力集中，不容易开小差，课堂氛围好 2）利于互动讨论，可以面对面交流 3）方便一边听一边做笔记 4）能得到同伴提示帮助	1）易受周围同学的影响 2）学生多，问题多时可能无法及时反馈 3）后排学生可能会看不清PPT内容，听不清老师讲解时来不及做笔记	1）促进学生自主学习，培养自主性 2）可以看录播和直播回放 3）人人可网上提问答疑 4）节省交通时间 5）整个教学生态（课件、资料、线上作业等）更丰富	1）没有老师的现场监督，受学习环境限制，自律性不强的同学课上容易溜号、开小差，跟不上教学节奏，从而导致学习效果差 2）无法面对面交流互动 3）面对屏幕上课眼睛容易疲劳	1）培养并加强学生的学习自主性和自律性 2）指导学生利用网络手段与同学和教师互动、沟通、交流、协作

	线下教学		在线教学		建议
	优点	弊端	优点	弊端	
教材	1）纸质书本居多，做题、记笔记方便 2）适合学生的学习习惯，翻阅书本比较方便	1）很多书本又厚又重，不方便携带，影响学习	1）可以使用电子教材，方便携带 2）可随时翻阅	1）在电子版教材上记笔记、做题不如纸质书本方便 2）对电子设备软件配备有成本要求	1）充分利用电子版教材的编辑、涂写和易于携带等功能及特点
教具	1）教师可近距离发挥（讲演、板书等）自身优势进行独立教学 2）有学校提供的教学资源 3）线下教学辅助工具丰富多样，易于开展各种课堂教学活动	1）受教具资源限制，有时个别学生参与教学活动会受影响	1）直播平台软件技术强大，提供的教具资源丰富	1）对直播平台和软硬件设备依赖性强 2）高配置软硬件设备有成本要求 3）对网速依赖性高 4）需要师生操作多项设备或软件	1）充分利用方便快捷、功能齐全的直播平台和软件实现即时、同步、高频的有效互动和输入
教法	1）灵活、生动、直观 2）针对性和互动性强 3）可讲授、讨论、表演，易于开展分层次、多样化的教学活动	1）签到、答题、评分等统计费时费力	1）可以利用丰富的网上教学资源 2）可实现一定程度的互动（如互评互改） 3）可进行即时网上反馈、统计、筛选问答	1）对软硬件设备和技术依赖大 2）互动方式和活动比较单一 3）对学生的自主性和积极性有更高要求	1）教师要通过适度开展网络有效互动，随时跟踪线上教学情况 2）丰富线上教学方式方法
教学内容	1）对教学内容掌控度比较高 2）会利用一部分线上资源	1）无法回放	1）可录播回放 2）教师可更充分利用网上技术和教学资源	1）教学资源过多，学生无法全部有效完成	1）根据学生特点设计不同时段的课程 2）给学生推荐适量有针对性的教学资源

注：部分观点来自学生，作者整理并补充。

从上表中可以看出，若能克服在线教学的弊端，比如互动性、生动性、针对性等的缺陷，发挥在线教学的自身优势，在线教学效果会大大提高。根据前文所述，教学中的有效可理解性输入、你来我往式互动是教学效果提升的关键，结合上表，除了本书论及的各个层面，教师在线教学还应在以下几个层面提升：

1）备人方面，应加强对学生学情的了解。相较于线下教学可以直接面对面了解学生的一举一动，教师对线上学生的了解更为困难。可以通过线上问卷整体了解学生状况，可以通过语音或视频对个别学生进行了解。根据学习者的年龄大小可选择与家长沟通，从而对教学对象有更充分的了解。

2）备物方面，教师应有针对性地加强网络软件和技术的学习，选好可靠稳定的平台和有效的教学软件，提高教学的即时、同步、高频互动。

3）备课方面，应加强课程的短、趣、快设计，除了要有目的地增加互动性外，尽量使课堂生动、灵活、有趣。根据学习者年龄等特点，要设计出不同时长的课程和课堂活动，激发并保持学生的学习兴趣。

Thoughts on Online Teaching

When teaching online, it is important that students feel connected and supported. There are two modes of doing this, synchronous and its opposite, asynchronous. Synchronous means the teaching and learning take place at the same point in real time, like when photos or documents are synchronized or synced onto different devices. Asynchronous teaching and learning occur when activities are set for students to do at their own choice of time.

Many classes have been conducted during the recent COVID-19 lockdowns across the world using a variety of synchronous platforms, such as Dingding, Tencent, Zoom, Skype, Teams, Google Hangouts and Adobe Connect.

Asynchronous learning has been facilitated by mini-lesson video recordings, google slides, documents and PowerPoint presentations being supplied to students through platforms such as Google classroom, Moodle, Chatgroups, Wiki blogs and ManageBac.

Anne Fox, an Intercultural Language Learning Online Facilitator with The Consultants-E Ltd, UK, stressed that when teaching online a teacher needs to be prepared to "Cut and Expand" a lesson plan. Generally, a teacher will not be able to cover as much material when teaching online. The students will quickly lose concentration, when they are required to simply look at the teacher on a screen. Many other distractions can be taking place around them in their home setting, that would not occur in a classroom. Consequently, the online lesson needs to have only one or two concise, clearly stated objectives with short activities that support them.

The focus of the teaching, whether it is synchronous or asynchronous, must be to maximize the interactions between the teacher and the student. Language learning is a social activity, but when students are required to be socially distanced, they must be given as many opportunities as are possible to communicate in the target language. This is particularly important when students are locked down in their homes with only opportunities to speak their home languages.

The synchronous lesson needs to allow for interactions between the students themselves as well as the teacher. This, of course, can be a challenge when the class size is large. Nevertheless, it is critical for students to communicate and practise their oral language skills. Remember, there is a sense that it is true that "Less is More". Less talking by the teacher can mean more thinking by the student.

In asynchronous learning, students will primarily be communicating through writing. This gives authentic purpose to their writing and can allow the teacher to analyse very quickly the type of grammatical errors that are most frequently occurring. Less assignments given may also mean more quality work is done. This can be another interpretation of "Cut and Expand".

The teacher needs to reach out to her students, but at the same time, this should not mean that the student and the teacher are connected every moment of the day. There must be a balance maintained between being there for your students and having time to refresh your body, mind and spirit.

Allison Yang and her colleagues at KIS, Bangkok, in March 2020, came up with the following, helpful poster, with what to do on the left and what NOT to do on the right side.

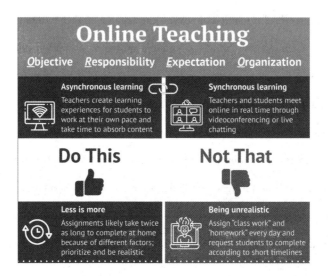

Give explicit instructions

Outline deliberate instructions and specify the length of time to complete the session of learning

Being unclear and vague

Communicate in lengthy paragraphs with instructions that may be difficult to follow or tasks that are overly vague

Specify expectations

Specify task requirements and length clearly (e.g. 2 minute audio recording with a bulleted checklist)

Being too open-ended

Assign tasks that are too open ended (e.g. make a video about the moon; write an essay about pollution)

Be empathetic

Assign a reasonable workload; encourage students to balance online with offline and connect with one another

Be overly task-oriented

Assign online classwork followed by extra homework without a clear focus on student wellbeing

Communicate consistently

All instructions and assignments **must** be communicated via ManageBac, our online hub

Mixed communication

Use multiple platforms inconsistently (e.g. email followed by Google Classroom w/ MB submission)

Be online for 'office hours'

Be online during office hours to provide support, answer questions, or clarify confusion via a *system*.

Stand by at all times

Respond to every email right away and leave no break for yourself (unless it's urgent, it can wait until office hours)

Seek student feedback

Seek student feedback about their workload, emotional state, learning preferences, and learning pace

Use the same approach

Teach in a way that does not give students voice and/or choice, leaving them feeling overwhelmed

Boost learning retention

Curate multimedia materials to boost learning retention and use digital tools to create interactive lessons

Try new & unused tools

Trying new tools that you've never used may lead to technological difficulties and increase challenge

Identify lesson objectives

Be intentional and identify clear learning objectives and assessment outcomes (formative and summative)

Give random activities

Keep students busy doing online activities and do not think about the lesson objectives and assessments

小结、反思与练习

Summary, Reflection and Practice

本章简要回答了几个常见的问题：

☐ 外语学习和二语学习是两回事，原版教材的使用应有所调整或改编；

☐ 能进行有效的语言沟通最重要；

☐ 英语早学有理论根据，习得要比学习效果好，但是要注意有效输入；

☐ 词汇量的大小固然重要，但关键点在于要和孩子进行有意义的互动；

☐ 线上学习与线下学习各有优势，要达到好的效果一定要注意可理解性输入，与孩子进行有意义的互动；

☐ 在线教学应尽可能实现即时、同步、高频为特点的互动，力争教师少讲、学生多动（Less is More），达到教的少、学的多（Cut and Expand）。

小结 Your summary

1.

2.

3.

反思 Reflection

1. The most effective way for language learning is ...

2. One thing I could do to improve myself is ...

3. One thing I could do for fun is ...

练习 Practice

1.

2.

3.

教研团队练习 Group Discussion：

1.分组讨论教学准备（Discuss）

2.分组进行案例分享（Share）

3.分组开展讨论应用（**Apply**）

初 心 与 结 语
First and Final Thoughts

爱是教师教育的第一心法
Love is Everything in Teaching

1. 初心First Thoughts

从事教学的初心是什么？这是每个从业者都该时不时问自己的问题。教师是一个高要求的职业，因为教师远不止是传授知识、培训技能、答疑解惑、教书育人，教师要扮演的角色很多。

What is your first thought or reason for being an English teacher? If people do not ask and reflect upon why they choose their lines of work, they may lose their way eventually. Being a teacher is really a demanding and challenging job. While people may think it is not easy to teach, to educate, to discipline, to answer questions and solve problems, they are correct. But these things are only part of the trials of teaching. Teachers play a dozen roles while teaching.

为了简明扼要，本书围绕课前、课中和课后展开。相关教学故事随文呈现，娓娓道来，各种可供参考且实用的教学模板如教学目标、教案设计、检查单、报告单、档案袋、示例图表等也一一奉上。

For the purposes of this book, teaching is considered as a three-step activity even though it is more than that. The first step consists of activities-planning and preparation, which are required to be done as much as possible before teaching. The second step occurs within the classroom and involves classroom management, teaching and learning. The third step takes place after teaching and includes communication and assessment with associated activities such as talking, interviewing, calling, checking, testing, evaluation and reporting either in written form or in an oral style.

不管以什么缘由从事教师这个职业，请记住教师的核心原则：爱、尊重、耐心、鼓励、安全、沟通。

However, for this chapter, we would like to talk about guiding thoughts before entry into the teaching field. Some teachers regard teaching as a job, some see it as their career, others might be lost in between. No matter how you think of it, always remember to love your students and respect them.

Story 22 : Love Your Students

Every child is unique. Their personalities, ways of thinking and attitude to life all combine to make each one an individual. Yet we often teach them all in the same way. Nevertheless, our interactions with each human being must be personal, letting them know that they are valued for who they are.

One of my students had a prosthetic leg, having been born with only one leg and a short stump where the second leg should have been. At the age of six to seven, this young man was becoming more aware of his differences compared to other boys of his age. Sometimes, he was easily upset by what another student had said on the playground. Yet, he could climb up the fortress play equipment as quickly as anyone else. He ran races to the best of his ability, cheered on by the students and teachers at the school.

One day while the class was on an excursion to a Water Park, he left me holding his prosthetic leg, as he ran (hopped and crawled) to play without it. He had nonchalantly taken the leg off as I held his clothes bag. At the end of the water fun, he changed and adeptly put the leg back on without any assistance from me.

His mother once wrote expressing her thanks to me not only for the ESL teaching, but also for the emotional and physical care I gave to him at school.

爱学生，爱每一个学生。

We are the apple of our parents' eyes; therefore, also keep in mind that every child is the apple of their parents' eyes.

Story 23 : 27 Ping Pong Balls

One day, I was at the school's annual swimming carnival with my Year One class of twenty-seven five-year-old children. The children had enjoyed their different races and were happily enjoying some free time in the water. I had to watch with an eagle eye to ensure every child was safe and happy. The school principal came by and stood by me watching the children as well. I will never forget his comment that day. "Janienne, your job of teaching these children is like trying to keep twenty-seven ping pong balls under water at the same time."

How true that statement was, as in those days, I did not have any teacher aide assistance, but had to manage the education, care and safety of all these young lives. It was physically and mentally demanding but the rewards of seeing the children develop, made it all worthwhile.

作为教师，不仅仅是教书，更是育人，当然也包括照顾学生的身心健康安全!

Being a teacher means more than just teaching, as people usually believe; it also means taking care of the students mentally, spiritually and physically.

Teaching can consume every moment of our days; however, it can be a most rewarding vocation if we put our heart and soul into it. This is why the profession of teaching can be one of the greatest occupations of all. Some children require a lot more effort and support. This is where the professionalism of the teacher becomes evident.

Story 24 : Writing A Long Name

A young boy, who had just arrived from China, joined my class at an international school. He could only speak and write in Chinese, having no English language skills, while I had very little Chinese language skills.

Proudly he wrote his name in Chinese characters. However, I could not read Chinese characters and neither could the other teachers with whom he would interact. It was time to teach him to write his name using the English alphabet.

It was not easy because his name in Pinyin had nine letters for him to learn. Every lesson I dotted his name for him to trace onto the correct lines. I provided him with a name card for him to copy. He wrote his name using different media, such as coloured pencils, whiteboard pens, even play dough and sand, practising every day. He had to identify the missing letters in another activity. Finally, after a few weeks he could successfully write his name in English. We celebrated the achievement with a special certificate.

爱、尊重、耐心与鼓励是我们帮助孩子成长必需的专业素养。

Patiently, I used my professional skills to carefully guide this young boy's progress with encouraging love and respect.

资深教师Rita Pierson在TED演讲中曾这样说，"Kids don't learn from people they don't like"（孩子们不会跟他们不喜欢的人学习）。孩子们喜欢你，你的教学效果也就成倍增长。只有爱孩子的老师才有可能成为高效能教师。爱孩子，尊重他们，聆听他们，他们自然也会认真聆听你。

爱、尊重、耐心、鼓励，这些都是高效能教师的必由心法、专业素养。其中，爱是教师的第一心法，一切之源。

Love, respect, patience and encouragement are the engines and real essences of being a highly effective teacher.

2. 结语 Final Thoughts

Every day in the classroom, we encourage our students to be thinkers as they explore the world around them and grow in their learning. As effective educators, we should also be thinkers, constantly evaluating our teaching.

While we plan lessons, we need to be considering what will work best for the students we have at that moment. Just because a lesson was effective in a previous year or in another class, doesn't mean that it will be effective for another group of students with different needs and at different places in their language learning.

During a lesson, an effective teacher will be questioning whether a particular activity is working and perhaps be thinking about how to change it to maximize its impact. Sometimes a wise teacher will abort an activity, if they consider that it is not achieving its desired outcome.

After a lesson, we must assess whether our teaching served its purpose. Asking questions of ourselves is necessary if we are to keep on improving our teaching. Such questions include: What was good about that lesson? What could have been done better? Why didn't that work? Was it the children who were at fault or was it me?

A competent teacher must be prepared for hard work. The teaching career is not for the lazy person, for it involves the whole intellect all through the day and often every ounce of strength and energy as you interact with excited young learners.

Nevertheless, the rewards are well worth it. As a child's curiosity is captured, you will share with them in their joy of learning. Therefore, enjoy every moment of being an effective teacher.

致 谢

Acknowledgments

本书从构思至定稿历时四年，目标一直很明确，就是想为中小学及幼儿英语教师，尤其是新手教师提供一本简单、有趣、实用的"傻瓜机"式的工具，让小白快速成长为高手，成为高效能教师。

虽然初衷如此，但并没有什么成功教学的万能钥匙。若是有的话，那应该就是热爱与勤奋。因为，教师教育容不得一丝怠惰，教学不仅仅只是教书本上的知识，在我们鼓励并教育学生探索世界和思考时，我们首先要成为思考者和探索者；在为孩子们设计每一节课的时候，我们就成为了有设计思维的设计师；在教学过程中我们要随时根据教学进展情况做出判断和取舍，因此我们又必须是敏锐的引导人和果断的决策者；"吾日三省吾身"般的教学反思，使我们天然地养成反思的习惯；"学高方为人师"又让我们成为终生的学习者……这一切来得那么自然而又伟大，只因我们哺育和启迪的是一个个鲜活的生命和灵魂……

衷心感谢家人！没有她们的支持，这本书不可能完成。

非常感谢Ace，感谢他一直以来的信任！

十分感谢ACD学术部负责师资培训和教学质量的SHEL教师培训师团队与其他专职和兼职的培训师，以及所有接受培训的教师学员们！是她们的青春激扬和积极努力给了我莫大的启发和支持！

最想感谢的是学生们，是他们的稚嫩可爱和时有的淘气，让我们重新不断地认识教育和爱，教育之本始于心之教育（*The heart of education begins from the education of the heart*）。愿每一位教师——心灵的园丁，成为幸福之源，播撒爱的种子，激励爱的灵魂，培育爱的天使。

据说，教育就是一棵树摇动另一棵树，一朵云推动另一朵云，一个灵魂唤醒另一个灵魂。（*The essence of education means that one tree shakes another tree, one cloud pushes another cloud, and one soul awakens another soul.*）真诚地感谢他们，感谢那些摇动、推动、唤醒我们的每一棵树、每一朵云、每一个灵魂。

限于水平，虽竭尽全力，数易文稿，但总难免挂一漏万。在此，诚恳地邀请读者给予批评指正，以便我们修订完善。

愿我们也能摇动树、推动云、唤醒灵魂，一起更好地践行最有爱的教育。

丁仁仑、珍妮·沃恩

2020年5月8日

于中国杭州、新加坡

读者问卷

阅读本书后您的收获是：

1.

2.

3.

阅读本书后您近期的主要目标是：

1.

2.

3.

您对本书的宝贵建议：

1.

2.

3.